BURPEE

AMERICAN GARDENING SERIES

ROSES

Suzanne Frutig Bales

Prentice Hall Gardening

New York · London · Toronto · Sydney · Tokyo · Singapore

This book is dedicated to my daughters, Margaret Meacham and Cathryn Bales who share my love of roses.

PRENTICE HALL GENERAL REFERENCE
15 Columbus Circle
New York, New York, 10023

Library of Congress Cataloging-in-Publication Data

Bales, Suzanne Frutig.
    Roses / Suzanne Frutig Bales.
        p.   cm.—(Burpee American gardening series)
    Includes index.
    ISBN 0-671-85044-X
    1. Roses.   2. Rose culture.   I. Title.   II. Series.
SB411.B335   1994
635.9'33372—dc20   92-43069
                                                    CIP

Designed by Levavi & Levavi
Manufactured in the United States of America
10 9 8 7 6 5 4 3 2 1

First Edition

Acknowledgments
    I would like to express my gratitude to the many people who have helped me. My thanks go to my husband and best friend, Carter; my gardening partner, Martha Kraska; and my assistant, Gina Norgard for providing me with unending help and support. Robert Sabin (and his garden) has been an inspiration as he has taught me his methods of growing roses and provided photos for this book. Many thanks also go to Beverly Dobson, one of America's leading authorities on roses, who lent her expertise and reviewed the manuscript.
    The American Rose Society and the Long Island Rose Society assisted me in my research. I especially want to thank Robert Ardini, Esther Jasik, Robert Titus and Ellen Minet. Thanks also to the people whose rose gardens appear in this book: Dorothy Hirshon, Kathy Heyes, Sherran Blair, Bob Titus, Adele Mitchel, David Dawn and Carol Mercer.
    Rayford Reddell and Robert Galyean graciously shared their knowledge in their book, Growing Good Roses and allowed me to photograph at their Garden Valley Ranch.
    At W. Atlee Burpee & Co. I would like to thank Barbara Wolverton and Elda Malgieri. At Prentice Hall Gardening I am indebted to Rebecca Atwater and Rachel Simon.
    Again, as in my other books, I want to thank my father who graciously gave freely of his time to help me shape the book.

PHOTO CREDITS
Agricultural Research Service, USDA: pp. 92–93; All-America Rose Selections: p. 68 top; Haring, Peter: pp. 64 bottom, 77 top; Jasik, Esther: p. 80 top right; Rokach, Allen: p. 33; Sabin, Robert: pp. 64 top and middle, 65 top, 66 top, 67 bottom right, 72 bottom; Scanniello, Stephen: page 58; W. Atlee Burpee & Co.: p. 69 bottom.

Illustrations on pages 36–37 by Pamela Kennedy
Illustrations on pages 41 and 85–86 by Michael Gale.

*Cover: White 'Mme. Hardy', coral pink 'Ferdy' and mauve 'Tour de Malakoff' are in bloom
on the author's bank of old roses.*

*Preceding page : A fragrant garden of tree roses (Rosa
'Tournament of Roses') with lavender at their feet. In
the container, miniature roses are combined with lamb's ear.*

CONTENTS

INTRODUCTION

Celebrities come and go in my garden, some better behaved than others. Over the years, 'Elizabeth Taylor', 'Ingrid Bergman' and 'Dolly Parton' have each visited. 'Mister Lincoln' and 'Queen Elizabeth' have always lived here.

Whether it be singer, movie star or president, I have always found it difficult to resist a rose named after a favorite personality. Those who sell roses know America's weakness for celebrities, so beware of the names of roses. They conjure up all kinds of favorable images that appeal to our imaginations. Roses have been named after Shakespearean characters ('Othello'), presidents ('Mister Lincoln' and 'John F. Kennedy'), queens ('Queen Elizabeth'), country-and-western singers ('Patsy Cline' and 'Dolly Parton'), luxuries ('Penthouse'), automobiles ('Chrysler Imperial') and cupcakes ('Twinkie'). 'Broadway' and 'Las Vegas' are as glitzy and gaudy as their namesakes.

Even cute clichés ('Teeny Bopper') and television shows ('Good Morning America') are out there. But there's no duplication. The number of new roses introduced increases, and each rose, like any racehorse, must first have its name researched and registered to assure it is the only one so named.

A beautiful rose, whether in bud with its promise of a flower or in full bloom, is difficult to resist. Who is unmoved by the beauty of roses? They are the most widely grown of all flowers, and rightly so, as they set a standard of beauty, vigor and scent unmatched by any other plant family. There is no denying that with these intricate and delicate flowers you have it all. In number of flowers and length of bloom, roses outbloom every other plant. Their virtues include exceptional color, beauty, charm and fragrance. Their allure is legendary. They have been the subject of poets and the symbols of love, yet they can be grown by anyone. There is a rose for everyone.

I have never heard it said that there are too many roses, but so it seems to me when I am trying to choose only one to grow in a small garden. The choices are daunting. In this book, my prejudices and favorites have crept into my advice, just as yours will be seen in your garden. Remember, each rose has its faults, just as each rose has its strengths, even those that bloom only once. (More about that later.) If possible, don't select roses from photographs alone. Check with your local nursery, rose society and botanical garden for specific recommendations on which roses grow best in your area.

As much as I love roses, I do not grow them to the exclusion of other flowers, nor am I a collector of plants without regard for the overall effect. I'm a flower lover, gardening for fragrance and beauty. I derive pleasure from sitting in the garden and, weather permitting, I eat every summer meal outdoors. So to me, garden presentation is most important. Many a time, caught unexpectedly by the beauty of the sunlight on a rosebush or the glow of colors as the sun sets, I have been cheered.

I presently grow more than 300 roses. They are mixed into flower beds and displayed in a formal rose garden; they serve as hedges, dutifully support a steep bank, and climb on the house, up trellises and over fences. I hope to debunk a few myths while teaching the basics of good rose culture, sometimes explaining both sides of a controversial issue. No matter how expert the rosarian, his or her advice can go only so far toward improving another's garden. Always and in all gardens, common sense is the most useful tool of all.

I started out as a dutiful gardener, following accepted "rules," only to discover, as Katharine Hepburn has said, "If you obey all the rules you miss all the fun." The only real path to knowledge is experience, and experience means breaking a few rules, trying new methods, exchanging ideas with other gardeners and reading a variety of books. Only then can you judge for yourself which roses to grow and how to grow them. That is truly where and when the fun begins.

Whimsically named the "electric garden seat" for the jolt of color and fragrance it delivers, this resting spot entices the visitor with climbing roses: pink 'Aloha', yellow 'Golden Showers', red 'Don Juan', and multicolored 'Joseph's Coat'.

THE ROSE GARDEN PLANNER

PLANNING FOR FRAGRANCE

How do you describe the fragrance of a rose? It is as difficult as describing the flavor of chocolate to someone who has never tasted it. One might say roses have a floral fragrance, mostly true in the old roses. But roses with their complex ancestry have a mix of fragrances frequently compared to fruits, herbs, spices, tea, myrrh, anise-licorice, honey, violets and even medicines. These "flavors" are commonly used to describe a rose's scent.

Many new rose introductions bred by David Austin are reputed to smell like myrrh. How does anyone know what myrrh smells like? As far as I know, it was last heard of traveling by camel with the three wise men. Having smelled roses, I find myrrh's perfume sweet with a medicinal punch. The tea fragrance, while identifiable by virtually all the experts, is controversial. Peter Beales, widely recognized as an authority on old roses, wrote in his *Classic Roses*, "[I] have yet to detect any real resemblance to the scent of tea in any of [the roses]." Be that as it may, there is a distinct scent (sweet, to me, with a light kick) categorized as a "tea" fragrance by rosarians. To learn to distinguish among roses you'll have to smell a lot of them.

As if this were not complicated enough, the perfume of some roses changes as they open and age. Each rose fragrance is made up of a combination of compounds present in the oil of the rose. Some compounds evaporate more quickly than others and, as they do, the rose's scent changes. For example, when it first opens, 'Crimson Glory' has a floral "rose" fragrance, but an older, open rose on the same plant will have a spicy clove smell. 'Peace', one of the most popular roses, opens with almost no fragrance and after a few days has a pungent, spicy scent similar to nasturtium. Not all roses have a pleasant fragrance. The wet leaves of *Rosa xanthina* and *R. ecae* have been documented as smelling like an anthill or formic acid. 'Sunsprite' and a number of other yellow roses have a fragrance similar to licorice, loved by some and repugnant to others.

Today's roses are not, as is commonly thought, universally fragrant; in fact many are scentless. Fragrance is a recessive trait and two deeply fragrant parents could, and often do, produce a scentless offspring. The pink and red roses are the most highly scented while white and yellow roses are rarely fragrant. Since the scent of most roses is mainly in the petals, it follows that the double roses are more fragrant, although the quantity and quality of the scent varies greatly with the rose. As they dry and wither, most rose petals lose their perfume while holding their color. Only the 'Apothecary's Rose' is known to hold its fragrance after drying. (As rose petals are the main ingredient in many potpourris, their fragrance needs to be refreshed with drops of essential oils.) Exceptions are the musk rose, with fragrance in the stamens, and the eglantine rose, with most of its fragrance in its foliage rather than the flower petals.

The climbing rose 'America' dresses Robert Titus' barn with her finery.

Fragrance is fickle and varies with the weather. It is most pronounced and travels farthest on days that are warm and moist. Some warm and misty mornings I awake to the fragrance of roses wafting in my upstairs window. On other days the excessive heat and drought of summer repress the scent of the roses, and wandering through the garden, I find their fragrance is barely perceptible. The same is true on cold, cloudy days, when the fragrance of all roses decreases. Fragrance flourishes following a summer shower and after a light frost.

To capture fragrance and enjoy the pleasure it brings takes planning. If well planned, a rose garden can be a rich blend of fragrances. If we bend over a little and stop and sniff more often, we can increase our enjoyment of our gardens. Some roses flaunt their fragrance, flooding the garden with enticing scents that, as the old saying goes, "could embalm a statue." Other roses bury their perfume deep in their petals, coaxing us closer to breathe their essence as they share their perfume only with our bowed heads. A rose in the middle of a wind tunnel will lose its fragrance to the wind. In a protected corner, a rose on either side of a garden seat breathes its perfume toward seated guests. An arbor of roses is a perfumed passageway. Inside a gazebo smothered in fragrant roses the air is perfumed most delightfully. Plant roses under windows that are open in summer, and enjoy their perfume both indoors and out.

Picked in the early morning and brought into the house, roses will be more fragrant. Their perfume isn't dissipated by drying breezes. A bowl of Damasks, gallicas or noisettes will bring the best of the rose floral fragrance indoors. Even one exquisitely perfumed rose such as 'Mister Lincoln' or 'Don Juan' in a slim vase can change the atmosphere of a room. To really understand a rose's fragrance you have to live with it and get to know its perfume in your garden as well as in your house.

Here are some roses grouped by fragrance families.

FRUIT FRAGRANCE

'Abraham Darby'—fruity
'Angel Face'—fruity
'Buff Beauty'—pineapple-
    banana
'Cerise Bouquet'—raspberry
'Gold Medal'—apple
'Hawaii'—raspberry
'Honorine de
    Brabant'—raspberry
'Madame Isaac
    Pereire'—raspberry
'Medallion'—fruity
'Nymphenburg'—sweet apple
'Parson's Pink China'—lemon
'Pinocchio'—fruity
Rosa mulliganii—ripe
    banana
Rosa wichuraiana—green
    apple
'Soleil d'Or'—cheap imitation
    of an orange, artificial
'Sutter's Gold'—fruity
'White Lightnin'—citrus

'Graham Thomas' is a long-blooming, modern English rose with the fragrance of old roses.

MYRRH FRAGRANCE

'Constance Spry'
'Fair Bianca'
'Sun Flare'
'Wife of Bath'

OLD ROSE FRAGRANCE
(originated with the
Damask roses)

'Fashion'
'Gertrude Jekyll'
'Intrigue'
'Mary Rose'
'Penelope'
'Othello'
'The Reeve'®
'The Squire'

TEA FRAGRANCE

'Buff Beauty'
'Candy Stripe'
'Charlotte Armstrong'
'Color Magic'
'English Garden'
'Fragrant Cloud'
'Gloire de Dijon'
'Graham Thomas'

'Kordes' Perfecta'
'Miss All-American Beauty'
'Oklahoma'
'Perdita'
'Royal Highness'

SPICY FRAGRANCE (usually
suggestive of anise or cloves)

'Angel Face' (listed as fruity
as well)
'Bewitched'
'Christopher Stone'
'Crimson Glory'
'Double Delight'
'Étoile de Hollande'
'Fru Dagmar Hastrup'
'Little Darling'
'Mirandy'
'Roseraie de l'Hay'
'World's Fair'

SWEET FRAGRANCE

'Sheer Bliss'
'Showbiz'
'Summer Fashion'
'Voodoo'

While many modern roses have lost their scent through extensive breeding, 'Fragrant Memory' is a hybrid Tea rose with an unforgettably sweet fragrance.

PLANNING FOR COLOR

Color affects a garden's mood and reflects the gardener's taste. Roses are available in colors to satisfy meek and aggressive personalities alike. Some are bold enough to make you flinch while others soothe, quietly restoring peace to the frantic pace of today's world. The classic, timeless beauty of soft colors provides a peaceful, often romantic spot in the garden. On the other hand, roses in outspoken colors, in the hottest of shades, set the garden afire.

Pastels as a group work well together. Bold, bright colors, such as orange, red and yellow punch it out, each holding its own. But combine pastel pink with a bold, sunny yellow and trouble begins. The yellow will stand out and steal the quiet beauty of the soft pink. If noticed at all, the pink appears washed out and drab. A medium pink would brighten the soft pink and add a reflected blush to the soft pink petals.

An assortment of pinks punctuated by red works where the red is intended to be the center of attention, and pinks the backdrop. Red, however, comes in many shades. Mixing an orange-red with a scarlet could cause them both to shriek. Red and white always work together, as do pink and white. White roses reflect the moonlight and glow at twilight, while combining well with all colors.

To create depth and the appearance of a larger garden, place light pinks toward the outside and the reds and hotter

At Old Westbury Gardens, on Long Island, an old-fashioned, white climbing rose is trained on a chain at the back of the perennial border.

This view looks through an arbor of roses into the author's herb garden, where four 'Simplicity' roses are the main attraction. 'Simplicity' is very resistant to disease and doesn't need chemical sprays to stay healthy.

shades toward the inside of rose beds. The reverse, reds on the outside and lighter colors on the inside, will make the area appear smaller. If you prefer an assortment of colors, plan the placement of each rose's neighbor as judiciously as you plan the colors in your outfit for a night out on the town.

Fiery Foliage and Ornamental Hips

A rose is not just a pretty face. The beauty of the foliage of some roses and their ornamental hips—the fruit and seeds of the rose—outshines their flowers. Rosebushes are more than flowers. *Rosa glauca* (formerly *R. rubrifolia*) is grown for its burgundy leaves washed with silver and its hips that begin in early summer as dark burgundy and ripen to bright orange. The unusual silver-burgundy leaves

of *R. glauca* complement other, green-foliaged plants. Their fleeting flowers, Pepto-bismol pink, don't distinguish the bush.

Cool fall nights set many rosebushes afire with leaves in shades of red, yellow and orange, mingled with bright ornaments of red or orange hips. Few autumn shrubs share their beauty so generously. Hips form on old-fashioned species and some shrub roses as well as on modern roses. Single-flower roses and one-time bloomers generally produce colorful, ornamental hips. As with every other rose characteristic, rose hips vary. They stay on the shrubs for many months. They may be small, medium or large, smooth or prickly. Oval, round or flagon shaped, they appear in assorted shades of red, yellows, oranges and dark burgundy. The large bottle-shaped hips of *Rosa moyesii* are bright orange-red and as beautiful in the autumn landscape as the berries of any colorful fall shrub. *R. rugosa* is known for its cherry-tomato-like hips, the first ones forming in early summer; the flowers continue to bloom until fall, a time when hips and flowers decorate the shrub side by side. The small, red, oval-shaped hips of *R. eglanteria* and the pearl-sized red hips of *R. multiflora* hold their red color and decorate the bushes throughout the winter and into spring undamaged by the cold.

Brainwashed into deadheading roses immediately after bloom, I enjoyed the flowers of many roses while unaware of the beauty of their hips. If the

There is great variety in the shapes and sizes of rose hips, the fruit of the rose. The hips shown here are, clockwise from the top, 'Complicata', Rosa rugosa, R. moschata, R. glauca, 'Bonica' and the sweetbriar rose.

ROSES WITH ORNAMENTAL HIPS

ROSE	DESCRIPTION OF HIPS
'Fru Dagmar Hastrup'	large round, deep red
'Nymphenburg'	medium round, orange
'Penelope'	medium round, coral-pink
'Pink Meidiland'™	medium round, bright orange-red
Rosa eglanteria	small oval, orange-yellow
Rosa gallica	medium round, red
Rosa glauca	small round, orange
Rosa moyesii 'Geranium'	large flagon-shaped, red
Rosa multiflora	pearl-sized, red
Rosa roxburghii (chestnut rose)	large round, clear acid-yellow
Rosa rugosa	cherry-tomato-shaped and -colored
Rosa setigera (prairie rose)	small round to oval, red
'La Sevillana'™	medium round, scarlet

rose looks messy, as 'American Pillar' usually does, instead of cutting the dead flowers off, spray the petals with a strong water hose or pull the petals off to clean the bush, but don't cut the flowers or the hips won't form.

Pollination by bees is needed for hips to form. Heavy rainy weather when pollination is necessary results in less activity by bees, consequently fewer hips. If the hips are allowed to form on repeat-flowering roses, the gardener has fewer flowers, except in the case of the irrepressible rugosas. The formation of hips is a step of the natural cycle in a rose's life. Allowing hips to form on roses as frost approaches helps the rose slow its growth and prepare itself for its dormant period. A rose with hips will have greater winter hardiness and fewer cut stems open for pests and disease to enter.

ROSES WITH COLORFUL AUTUMN FOLIAGE

'Belle Poitevine'
'Blanc Double de Coubert'
'Hansa'
'Metis'
'Pink Grootendorst'
Rosa rugosa 'Alba'
Rosa spinosissima
Rosa virginiana

Rosa rugosa's autumn foliage puts on its own show, turning bright yellow in the frosty air to contrast beautifully with the red rose hips.

The large thorns on the climbing rose 'Aloha' hook onto anything near it to help it climb.

The once-blooming Rosa 'Geranium' is nearly thornless, making it easy for the gardener to prune the bush or pick the flowers.

Avoiding Thorny Problems

Thorns are not attributes appreciated by gardeners. Despite their small size, rose thorns grab and scratch the gardener. Most rosebushes are too thorny to be manageable without gloves. Even with the addition of heavily protective clothing for spring pruning, I finish my pruning chores looking like I attended an alley cat convention. I know of only one rose with beautiful thorns. The large, bright red thorns of Rosa omeiensis *var.* pteracantha *are closely spaced, decorating the length of the cane, dangerous when grabbed by the unwary but beautiful when caught by the rays of a bright sun. Beware, when placing roses, of putting them where they will constantly scratch passersby and admirers.*

Unlike the thorns of other shrubs, rose thorns do not grow out from the inside of the stem but are part of the epidermal cells or surface of the canes and therefore snap off easily. Many floral arrangers use thorn-stripping tools and remove the thorns before adding roses to an arrangement. While thorns are useful to the rose as a deterrent to predators (rabbits, deer and horses all find roses tasty treats), and climbing roses use them as handy hooks to catch on shrubs or trees to pull their branches closer to the sun, thornless roses (or, to be more accurate, nearly thornless roses) do exist in surprisingly large numbers. Yet, even the thornless roses, reverting to a former parent, occasionally send up a thorny cane or have a few prickles at the base of the plant. With only a few thorns, they are easier to get close to for pruning or picking than other roses. Along a narrow path, climbing over a porch, a gazebo or an area where children play, thornless roses can be perfect.

THORNLESS (OR NEARLY SO) ROSES

ROSE	CLASSIFICATION	COLOR AND FRAGRANCE
'Faint Heart'	Hybrid Tea	pink blend
'G Nabonnand'	Tea	coral/salmon*
'Kathleen Harrop'	Bourbon	light pink*
'Marie Pavie'	Polyantha	white*
'Mrs Dudley Cross'	Tea	yellow blend*
'Paul Neyron'	Hybrid perpetual	medium pink*
'Reine des Violettes'	Hybrid perpetual	mauve*
Rosa banksiae banksiae	Species	white*

GROWING ROSES FOR CUT FLOWERS

Worldwide, the three most important cut flowers are roses, chrysanthemums and carnations. Florist roses are very different from garden roses. They have been bred to grow in the greenhouse over the winter months, when demand is high in florist shops. The bushes have small foliage, so they take up little room in the greenhouse while producing many flowers. The flowers themselves are selected for the way they look in bud, not in full bloom like garden roses.

Rose Hills, a public garden with more than seven thousand rosebushes in 600-plus varieties located in Whittier, California, conducted a test to see which roses last longest in water without preservatives. The roses were all picked in bud as they were just beginning to unfurl and were placed in individual vases in a 72°F. room. Every two days the rose stems were recut and the water in the vase was changed. The favorite types of roses included hybrid Teas, floribundas, grandifloras and one climber. As a group, red, pink, and orange roses lasted longer in water than the whites and yellows. The fuller blooms with many petals took longer to unfurl and lasted longer than single roses.

When it comes to flower arranging there are of course advantages to long-stemmed modern roses, and I've never been anything but thrilled to receive them. They can be more easily used singly. They are at home in long-necked vases, elegant and romantic wherever they are placed. The loveliest, most traditional arrangements of roses are in silver or crystal, but pottery and china can also be beautiful in the right setting. Hybrid Teas are the aristocrats of the rose garden, making buxom bouquets. There are no rules when it comes to arranging roses. Do what pleases you.

I enjoy all roses indoors whether on long or short stems, and have yet to grow a type of rose I haven't cut and brought into the house. Some might say I'm not very discriminating, or perhaps always greedy for more, but I respect the rose's individuality and enjoy each variety. Mostly I find the hybrid Teas too fussy and formal, and love the globular blossoms of the cabbage rose and the ca-

Rose	Classification	Color and Fragrance
Rosa banksiae lutea	Species	medium yellow/ light yellow*
'Smooth Angel'	Hybrid Tea	apricot
'Smooth Lady'	Hybrid Tea	medium pink*
'Smooth Prince'	Hybrid Tea	medium red
'Smooth Velvet'	Hybrid Tea	dark red
'Thelma'	Rambler	pink blend
'Zéphirine Drouhin'	Bourbon	medium pink*

* strong fragrance

Even a simple arrangement of roses in a pitcher can be elegant. Pictured here is 'Lillian Austin', a fragrant, modern English rose bred by David Austin.

An arrangement of old roses combined with the perennials foxgloves and astilbe by floral designer J. Barry Ferguson is an exquisite centerpiece.

sual, coarse boldness of such rustic rugosas as the ruffled, fluted clusters of one of the Grootendorts. Squat vases stuffed to overflowing with old roses perfume the air and are more beautiful to me than the leggy, high pointed buds of hybrid Teas. Fishbowl shapes, teacups, chemist bottles, and other interesting containers are all appropriate for showing off the roses depending on the type of rose cut.

Roses mix well in bouquets with other flowers, although they may steal most of the attention. A gardener I know keeps ivy arranged in floral foam, draping over the edges of its bowl, and adds a few roses when guests arrive on short notice. The ivy, which looks good alone, becomes a backdrop that highlights the roses.

The romance of an arrangement appeals most when a few petals have dropped on the table. At times, when roses are looking disgruntled, I break them apart and scatter the individual perfect petals on the table to grace a casual dinner party. (Sometimes it is necessary to deter helpful people who want to clean them up before the guests arrive.) Or, the rose petals from fading roses—if not sprayed with chemi-

cals—nicely garnish entrées or desserts. Custards can float rose petals on their surface. Wedding cakes smothered in white rose petals or whole roses are romantic and beautiful.

LONG-LASTING ROSES FOR CUTTING: RESULTS FROM THE ROSE HILLS TEST

'America' (climber) — 5 days
'Bewitched' (hybrid Tea) — 6 days
'Cherish' (floribunda) — 4 days
'Color Magic' (hybrid Tea) — 4 days
'Deep Purple' (floribunda) — 7 days
'Duet' (hybrid Tea) — 5 days
'French Lace' (floribunda) — 5 days
'Gingersnap' (floribunda) — 5 days
'Gold Medal' (hybrid tea) — 7 days
'Honor' (hybrid Tea) — 5 days
'Iceberg' (floribunda) — 7 days
'Intrigue' (floribunda) — 4 days
'Marina' (floribunda) — 6 days
'Mister Lincoln' (hybrid Tea) — 5 days
'New Day' (hybrid Tea) — 6 days
'Olympiad' (hybrid Tea) — 9 days
'Paradise' (hybrid Tea) — 5 days
'Pascali' (hybrid Tea) — 8 days
'Prominent' (grandiflora) — 9 days
'Sonia' (grandiflora) — 9 days
'Summer Sunshine' (hybrid Tea) — 4 days
'Touch of Class' (hybrid Tea) — 9 days
'Viva' (grandiflora) — 8 days
'Voodoo' (hybrid Tea) — 8 days

Promiscuous Roses

Botanists and historians have sifted through the tangled genealogy of roses, but it is bewildering. The royal family of roses has been promiscuous since their very beginnings. Their history is a tale of intrigue, intermarriage and incest, the details long forgotten. So it shouldn't be too surprising that over millions of years, the rose family, through natural selection, mutations, chance seedlings, and planned and unplanned parentage has developed into distinct groups with new varieties coming faster all the time. People, of course, have fanned the flames in their insatiable desire for novelty and the search for the ever-better rose. Modern roses have interrelated lineage, developed from multiple crosses, re-crosses and back crosses. No wonder it is difficult to understand who fathered whom.

Roses have been part of cultures and civilizations since our earliest history. Fossil roses dating back at least 32 million years have been found in rocks of the Oligocene Epoch in Colorado and Oregon. It is widely believed roses originated in Central Asia and spread over the entire northern hemisphere, yet inexplicably, they never crossed the equator. Wild roses have been found growing far north in the arctic cold of Alaska and Siberia and as far south as the intense heat of India and North Africa.

Cultivation of roses dates back about five thousand years in China. Approximately two thousand years ago, just before the birth of Christ, the Han dynasty had huge parks devoted to roses. The parks grew roses even when food was scarce and agricultural lands were needed to feed the population. At about the same time, Egyptians grew roses for the Romans, exporting cut flowers to Rome by ship during the winter months. Even then in ancient Rome, structures heated with piped hot water were designed to force roses into bloom in December. During the decadent days of the Roman Empire, Romans stuffed their pillows and beds with rose petals, and showered confetti of rose petals on guests and used rosewater for bathing. Emperor Nero reportedly spent the equivalent of $160,000 in today's money on cut roses for one of his sumptuous banquets.

The sensuous appeal of roses is well known. Cleopatra, when entertaining Anthony, surrounded her bed with several feet of rose petals.

Following the fall of the Roman Empire, tainted by their association with its decadence and decline, roses slid out of favor. It wasn't until the 12th and 13th centuries that they again became socially acceptable, first for their use in medicines, and later for their beauty. The flower's scent was supposed to have had a healing influence, and the petals were used in making rosewater for flavoring unpleasant-tasting remedies and for bathing. But in all their popularity, only 14 kinds of roses were grown in the middle of the 14th century in England. (To modern science, the benefits in the flowers remain unfounded. Still, high content of vitamin C in the hips has proved higher than that in any common source; vitamin C is effective in the prevention of scurvy as well as the treatment of many diseases.)

Skipping through time, we arrive at the 19th century, when repeat-blooming roses from Asia landed in Europe, changing and expanding the existing breeding programs. The era of modern roses commences in 1867 with the introduction of 'La France', the first hybrid Tea rose. It was a haphazard creation and its story is a little fuzzy. It was discovered by Jean-Baptiste Guillot. Peter Beales wrote, "Guillot had no idea of its true parentage but concluded that it was the result of a secret liaison between one of his 'upper class' hybrid perpetuals and a Tea rose with a roving eye."

Wild roses grow in every state today, and in such diverse terrains as sand dune, prairie and woodland. There are roses that will grow naturally anywhere. The wild roses are genetically established through the rugged process of survival in the wild, in contrast to the genetically mixed and pampered hybrids grown in today's gardens.

DESIGNING WITH ROSES

The shape of the rose you select should fit the location. Tree standards, for example, are best in formal settings; cascading shrubs soften rigid lines, and upright roses draw attention to themselves with their aristocratic bearing. The climbers add visual depth to the garden area and increase the feeling of space by drawing the eye up to meet the sky. Try, where possible, a variety of roses with distinctive characteristics before gravitating finally—if ever—to only one kind. Proper placement is the key to enhancing a rose's strength and to enjoying its individuality. The more care used throughout the planning to coordinate color, time of bloom and location, the happier you and your garden will be.

A single type of rose can't be made to fit everywhere, but careful selection will prove to you that there is a rose for every place. Let common sense be your guide. Gardens are built over time and through trial and error. Roses should not stand out awkwardly. They should be part of the whole plan, whether it be for a modest garden or a grand landscape. If a rose isn't right for one spot, you can find another home for it.

ROSES ARE SHRUBS TOO

Roses need not be segregated, to live only with their own kind. An old garden rose, a shrub rose, old or modern, and a well-mannered floribunda such as 'Betty Prior' can be grown together in the landscape as successfully as any other flowering shrubs. Think of roses as shrubs and as bedding plants. Despite sharing the same family name, roses make up a very diverse group. Each class of roses plays a different role. There are roses that can be planted on a demanding site—a sandy beach, a steep bank, a roadside. There are roses for seasides with salty air and for cold winters.

Species, old-fashioned and shrub roses, any one plant of which costs less than a bouquet of roses, are the easiest to mingle in shrub borders. They provide for a colorful summer when interplanted with evergreens around the foundation of a house. They are glorious in bloom and when decorated with hips in fall and winter. Bare rosebushes, when backed by evergreens, obligingly recede into the background.

Shrub roses can be planted at the back of a flower garden with perennials and annuals mixed in front. Too seldom grown, old garden roses, blooming with hundreds of fragrant flowers (the world's most exquisite perfume) are as easy to care for as other shrubs. Don't slight them. Lilacs, azaleas, forsythia and camellias are all popular flowering shrubs, yet they bloom but once for a few weeks. Why then do we demand continuous bloom from our roses? No

Roses make ideal companions for perennials. Here, 'Golden Showers' and 'America' climb in the ivy
at the back of a flower border, and the miniature rose 'Red Sunblaze' is mixed in the front.

'Golden Wings' is a prolific bloomer with good disease resistance.

Often the center attraction of an herb garden, roses historically were grown for their supposed medicinal properties. Only a rose that doesn't require chemical sprays to stay healthy can be grown in the same area as plants that will be eaten.

At the American Rose Society's Garden in Shreveport, Louisiana, a bench is surrounded by pink 'Carefree Wonder' and 'Center Gold'.

one rejects a lilac. Even mildewed and lanky, they are accepted in the best of gardens, their faults overlooked. On the other hand, roses are expected to be elegant, spotless and perfect. Spoiled by the florist's flowers grown in controlled greenhouses, we ask the impossible of those grown in our gardens.

TREE ROSES

Tree roses, roses in their most elegant form, are not a naturally occuring class in themselves, but rather products of the grafter's art. Tree roses elevate the flowers so they bloom atop a straight, 2- to 5-foot stem. The shortest tree roses are fashioned from miniature rose varieties.

Tree roses come in a variety of forms. Some resemble lollypops; others look more like miniature weeping trees. Each type draws attention to itself because of its height. I planted several tree roses at the back of a rose border where they can be seen at eye level above the lower rose bushes. At home in containers, tree roses can decorate either side of an entrance or be placed in the middle of a flower border as accents to add height and color above the level of the other flowers.

Hybrid Tea tree roses can be pruned into "trees," each with one strong, straight stem developed and branching from the top, but usually a hybrid Tea is grafted instead onto the tall main stem of another rose. Two different hybrid Tea roses may be grafted to the top of a single stem for a look that tends to be odd rather than beautiful.

POPULAR HYBRID TEA TREE ROSES

'Angel Face'
'Double Delight'
'Fragrant Cloud'
'Fragrant Memory'
'Graceland'
'Honor'
'Mister Lincoln'
'Perfect Moment'
'Pleasure'
'Shining Hour'
'Tournament of Roses'
'Tropicana'

PETTICOATS FOR ROSES

All too frequently in rose gardens, bare expanses of soil are left between the roses, detracting from the flowers. Mother Nature abhors a vacuum. If we gardeners don't cover the ground under our roses, she parachutes in seeds to fill the void. The first to arrive, the dreaded weeds, are quick to germinate and could keep a gardener busy all season with their removal. Leave home for a week or two, especially if it's rainy, and on returning you'll be impressed by their quick, miraculous growth.

Two solutions, equally effective, solve this problem. One is to spread an organic mulch (with the added benefit of enriching the soil—see page 41), and the other is to plant groundcovers around and between the roses. For aesthetic reasons, I prefer the second choice. Plant in front of and even between rosebushes for the best overall effect. Many staunch rosarians vehemently differ, convicting companion plants before they are proven guilty of root competition, stealing moisture and robbing nutrients. I compromise, suggesting for hybrid Teas a 1- to 2-foot-high edging of plants, such as dwarf boxwood, liriope or lavender. All will edge a garden, hiding the bare soil between the roses. For other roses, companion plants are compatible if chosen wisely. Flowering groundcovers, like frilly petticoats, billow out and beautify the roses. The Queen of Flowers needs a few lesser subjects at her feet to look her best. In a corner garden I grow a clump of 'Betty Prior' roses underplanted with sweet alyssum. The fragrance of the sweet alyssum compensates for the absence of fragrance in 'Betty Prior' and at the same time adds a ruffle to her flowering skirt. In the center of my herb garden, four 'Simplicity' shrubs sit snugly on a rug of thyme and lavender.

Plants can be added to bloom before, with, and after the rose, extending the flower season of the garden. Shade-growing flowers such as *Dicentra* 'Luxuriant' or *Vinca minor* nestle harmoniously under a rose's skirts while sunny plants

At the inviting entrance to a vegetable garden, two tree roses of 'First Prize' are planted at the back of a flower border to rise above the garden's fence.

In the formal rose garden at Filoli Center in Woodside, California, boxwood hedges define the garden structure and pink wax begonias are planted as a groundcover at the base of the tree roses.

Chives, santolina, creeping thyme and artemisia grow at the base of 'Simplicity' roses.

An old yellow rose climbs the wall of ivy easily without a lot of help from the gardener. It adds depth and height to the flower border. Dianthus and peonies are shown in bloom.

grow at the skirt's edge. Aromatic herbs at her heels are reputed to discourage insects. Add early spring-blooming bulbs for a colorful garden prior to the roses' bloom. Glory-of-the-snow, snowdrops, squills and daffodils all are suitable for planting in a rose garden layered under groundcovers. Lilies, planted under the rose's outer ruffle, rise up through her skirts to bloom with the rose. Their upright spikes contrast nicely with roses that have arching branches.

By combining the two methods, you have the best combination for a healthy and beautiful garden. Mulch under the rose's skirt, to keep the area around her base clear of other roots, and plant ground-covers such as lavender, growing about a foot high, outside her skirt to screen the mulch from view. It is details such as these that make a considerable difference by adding the finishing touches to frame the roses.

Old roses are another story entirely. Raised, hybridized and nurtured by Mother Nature to be independent and fend for themselves, they are survivors. They can easily fit into any sunny area. Lilies, planted at the outskirts of their branches, will grow up and through their brambles, blooming with the roses. Perennials and annuals can be planted in front or between them and all will happily co-exist.

FAVORITE GROUNDCOVERS FOR PLANTING UNDER ROSES

COMMON NAMES	LATIN NAMES
Bellflower	*Campanula* species
Bleeding heart	*Dicentra* 'Luxuriant'
Catmint	*Nepeta* species
Corydalis	*Corydalis* species
Cranesbill	*Geranium* species
Lady's mantle	*Alchemilla* species
Lamb's ears	*Stachys byzantina, S. olympica*
Lavender	*Lavandula* species
Myrtle	*Vinca minor*
Pansies	*Viola × wittrockiana*
Pinks	*Dianthus* species
Strawberries	*Fragaria* species
Thyme	*Thymus* species
Violet	*Viola* species
Wormwood	*Artemisia* species

ROUGH-AND-TUMBLE ROSES AS GROUNDCOVERS

Roses whose natural inclination is to sprawl excel as groundcovers. Ramblers, such as *Rosa wichuraiana* with their long canes flat and flowing, will scramble down a bank. Miniatures such as 'Arizona Sunset' with their low, spreading habit, and shrubs such as 'White Meidiland' that are dense growers are excellent groundcover possibilities. Rugosas and hybrid rugosas, such as 'Max Graf', root as they travel, sending up new shrubs a few feet away and then filling the ground in between.

If you think of the way classic groundcovers such as pachysandra cover the ground, suppressing weeds and staying low, the term groundcover can be deceiving. Roses, more often than not, cover the ground with lush, billowing cushions. They won't completely suppress weeds unless a few inches of mulch are spread under their skirts. The versatility of roses is evident in one newer introduction, 'Alba Meidiland', which sprawls densely down my garden's bank while climbing an 8-foot pillar in a friend's garden. It is both a good climber and a good groundcover. Grown for either purpose, it is a long-flowering beauty.

When planting roses on a slope, don't just stick them onto the side of the hill. For a good start, carve out a small level shelf, prepare the soil, and plant the bush upright. A metal strip or a pile of rocks placed along the shelf edge keeps water and soil from washing away down the bank.

GROUNDCOVER ROSES

'Alba Meidiland'
'Bonica'
'Carefree Beauty'
'Carefree Wonder'
'Ferdy'
'Max Graf'
'Paulii'
'Ralph's Creeper'
'Red Cascade'
Rosa wichuraiana
'Scarlet Meidiland'
'White Meidiland'

Beauty Contests for Roses

Local rose societies sponsor competitions across the country. The blue ribbons in themselves don't account for the passion of competitors competing for the most coveted prize, "Queen of Show." Straight stems, balanced foliage and high, pointed centers are some of the qualities necessary for a show-stopping winner.

An exhibitor's garden is usually a garden not planned for overall beauty but for the most practical means of growing show quality blooms. After all, the bush never enters the competition. Visiting an exhibitor's garden a few days before a show is an interesting sight. Perfect buds are protected while they open, decked in styrofoam caps, or shaded by umbrellas from harmful winds, rain and the glare of the sun. Buds need to remain on the bush to open properly. At the show, the morning hours are spent "grooming" the blooms. This in itself is an art form. Manicure scissors trim discolored or frayed edges of petals, cotton swabs are gently forced between petals to pry open tight blooms, and soft rags polish and shine foliage. All this for the judge's critical eye. The challenges are great, requiring concentration and determination. The atmosphere is as intense as that of any competition I have witnessed, and the joy of the winners far exceeds the token blue ribbon prizes. To find out more about rose shows and how to enter, contact your local rose society or The American Rose Society.

Many roses make wonderful groundcovers, preferring to grow wider than they are tall. Pictured here is 'White Meidiland'.

'Bonica' is a landscape rose that blooms from early summer until after frost without the need for chemical sprays.

ROSE HEDGES

Rose hedges are an attractive way to divide a property, line a walk, accompany a fence, provide summer privacy, establish a wind break or mark a property line. The trick is in choosing the roses that will do the job you need done. Height, maintenance, winter appeal for northern areas, and length of flowering are all characteristics to be considered. Floribundas, with their clusters of flowers, are good choices for short-growing hedges to divide a garden. Shrub roses that grow with dense tangles of canes and hold their hips through the winter will be colorful and provide some privacy. Gener-

ally, formal hedges are made with modern roses and informal hedges use shrubs, species or old-fashioned roses.

For a hedge, select roses that are harmonious companions and share the same growth habit. Those that complement each other in shape of flowers and color can be grown together to make a tapestry hedge. Consider an informal, thorny tangle of rugosas or a formally clipped hedge of composed elegance using modern roses. The color of the roses will set the mood, whether you choose the quiet restained colors of old roses or the flamboyant riot of colors available in modern roses.

A hedge can be a single row of roses or, for a thicker, more private hedge, a double row, with the back row bushes planted in a staggered arrangement behind the front row. Each shrub should be placed close enough to the next shrub so that they grow into each other.

Prune hard the first year to encourage growth from the base of the shrub. You don't want a hedge with a bare bottom. Once-flowering roses can be pruned right after bloom and allowed to grow all summer. A straggly cane can be pruned for a better shape anytime.

SEASIDE GARDENING

Rose hips form on Rosa rugosa *all summer and fall. They are the size and color of cherry tomatoes when ripe.*

Roses that tolerate salty air and strong winds do well at the seashore. Most of the old roses can be planted on hillsides or in gardens near the sea, but only the rugosa family readily adapts to being planted on the beach. The rugosas' natural bushy habit provides a windbreak. Both rugosa flowers and hips are present from August on, brightened later by the fall foliage. The single-flowered varieties produce a plethora of hips, while the doubles are more reserved and present hips sparingly.

Decades before my family moved to our seaside home, rugosas had naturalized at one end of our beach. Because they sent out runners into pure sand, gathering nutrients from

piles of seaweed and beach grass washed at their feet, I mistakenly thought they survived easily in sandy soil. I dug many, transplanting them to the other end of the beach, hoping they would share their fragrance with the swimmers, but they were unable to live on their own when planted in unimproved sand.

Now I first pot the runners in good potting soil, place the pot in a shady area (sunshine distracts the plant into putting energy into flowering), and keep it well watered to help it produce good roots. After a month, I prepare a hole in the sand on the beach two or three times as big as the pot and fill it with topsoil, compost, and peat moss to give the plant a healthy start. Potted rugosas purchased from a nursery should also be planted this way. With no other care than this, they not only survive, they thrive. A good beginning sets them for life. Their roots continue to grow out into the sand, spreading and propagating new bushes without any problems. In more than 10 years, I have never watered, fertilized, sprayed or given them any support other than the basic beginnings of a healthy life, and they have graced me with abundant flowers, fragrance and beauty.

During one fall hurricane the rugosas held their breath for several hours under four feet of salt water. After the water receded, they showed no signs of struggle.

Rosa rugosa *roses are perfect for planting on a beach. If planted in good, enriched soil, they will send runners out into the sand and can tolerate drought and an occasional salt water bath.*

DESIGNING WITH CLIMBERS

There are many clever uses for climbers. I inherited a red climbing rose, the name of which I've never discovered. Its feet are firmly planted at the back of a mixed flower border, taking up practically no space. The rose blooms once in June high up above a window on a wall covered with ivy. The dark red practically jumps off the wall in contrast to the dark green, shiny background of dense ivy. As the flower petals fall, the vine recedes into the background, and if it has any disease, black spot or mildew most likely among them, I don't know about it because it is camouflaged by the ivy. And what would it matter, as the ivy and rose have a happy marriage, their lives intertwined and compatible for more than forty years.

Many times, when I pass a bare trellis, an empty pillar, a bald wall, an unattractive fence, I fancy I hear them crying out to me. The lament is always the same: "If only someone would adorn me with roses." The romance of climbing roses should not be underestimated. They take relatively little garden space, surprising considering the heights many of them reach. A climbing rose on a pillar is a sight too rarely seen in this country, and roses growing up into trees are even more rare. Climbing roses should be more freely used to adorn pillars, wreathe windows, straddle fences, camouflage ugly structures and drape trees with their flowering tresses. Even a handsome flower garden is more interesting with the finishing touch of a climbing rose bush in the background. Small yards surrounded by wooden fences are more attractive with the shorter-growing roses entwined about the slats or rails of the fencing.

A garden appears larger when flowers bloom vertically. Height adds a new dimension. What could bring more pleasure than sitting under a canopy of flowers? Think tall. Climbing roses, thankful for a place on a warm wall, smile down from the heights and it is impossible not to smile back. They are cordial characters, combining easily with other plants, and should not be ne-

'Lady Banks' rose, with her long limbs, easily climbs the pillars at the Birmingham Botanical Gardens.

Cathy Heyes grows roses at the edge of her front lawn to decorate the picket fence. The pink rose is 'Charles Austin', a modern English rose, and its companion 'Buff Beauty' is a hybrid musk rose from 1939.

glected. Ramblers, climbing roses with longer canes, are seldom seen today but are worth seeking out. The flirtatious ramblers flaunt their blooms as they shamelessly enrapture anything close by, and gentle guidance is needed to curb them into appropriate behavior. Once you show them the way, they will surprise you with their ingenuity. One 'American Pillar' rose I planted to cover a chimney did much more than that. It covered the chimney, then sent one cane around the corner to create a sweeping floral hanging on the other side. I could never have imagined a more perfect path. The house was clothed in ivy and the rose clung to it as it wandered wherever it wished. It was lovelier than if I had told it what to do. One rambler, 'Lady Banks' rose, is nicknamed "house eater" for its proclivity to climb up a roof and dangle flowers over the other side. The best climbers for a bold display bloom but once a season. Frequently they wait until their second year to bloom, and bloom better on the previous year's growth. The impact of climbers, whether they be short or tall, does more to beautify a garden with its finishing touch than almost anything else. Even the smallest garden benefits from growing taller. When next in your garden, look up. Isn't there something that could be enlivened by the colorful robes of a rambler?

The shorter climbers can serve as curtains for garden rooms. A climbing rose covers quite a large area when fanned out to be equally as wide as tall. Bloom proliferates on horizontally trained canes where they receive more sun. Otherwise, they reach straight for heaven with bloom only on the top.

Climbers don't have to be planted only at the back of a garden. They dress up any dull area. The great variety of climbers and ramblers makes them a versatile group. They can be trained to cover arbors where they will surround the casual stroller with a delightful fragrance. A garden seat with a canopy of roses trained overhead creates a restful, fragrant and shady spot to welcome the weary. Windows crowned with wreaths of roses decorate the outside of a house, and fragrance floats inside when the windows are open. Ugly, bare walls and dull fences disappear when festooned with roses. A garden gate with a trellis of roses over the top is an invitation to enter. A tall fence decorated as a screen of roses handsomely divides two outdoor areas. Many ramblers will successfully scramble over an embankment, and prevent erosion as they grow and bloom with little or no care.

All climbers can lend their strong canes for the support of others. In my garden, 'New Dawn' and 'Aloha' not only harbored birds' nests this season, but served as trellises for other vines. Once a climbing rose is well established, its strong canes easily support weaker climbing vines. A large-flowered clematis (the small-flowered clematis usually grow too densely), morning glory, love-in-a-puff and other flexible-stemmed vines add blossoms to the climber later in the summer.

CLIMBERS 5 TO 10 FEET TALL

'Aloha'
'America'
'Don Juan'
'Eden Climber'
'Golden Showers'
'Joseph's Coat'
'Margo Koster'
'Rhonda'

CLIMBERS AND RAMBLERS 10 TO 20 FEET TALL

'Blaze Improved'
'Climbing Etoile de Hollande'

'Climbing Peace'
'Constance Spry'
'Dortmund'
'Gloire de Dijon'
'New Dawn'
'Zéphirine Drouhin'

CLIMBERS AND RAMBLERS TO 20 FEET TALL

'Belvedere'
'Bobbie James'
'Excelsa'
'Kiftsgate'
'Lawrence Johnston'
'Leontine Gervais'
'Paul's Himalayan Musk Rambler'

Clematis 'Hagley's Hybrid' is a beautiful sight draping over Rosa 'White Meidiland' here. Vines with flexible stems are easily supported by the strong canes of most roses.

Climbing 'Blaze' intertwines at the top of a window with an unnamed red rose. In front of the window, foxgloves bloom above the foliage of a tree peony and behind Lychnis coronaria *and forget-me-nots.*

Rosa 'Tausenchon' climbs on wires secured to the brick gazebo at Old Westbury Gardens.

DESIGNING WITH MINIATURE ROSES

When designing a garden with miniature roses it is important to situate them where their size is appropriate. In many gardens they look out of place because they are out of scale with the other plants. Miniatures can add a ribbon of color to the border of a flower garden or they can be mixed directly into the bed. Pots of miniature roses can be buried in the ground, their rims flush with the soil level, if root competition is a concern or if you'd like to bring them indoors easily to continue blooming longer into fall. If planted with perennials and annuals, they may need more fertilizer and water to compete with their neighbors, but they needn't be planted so far apart that there are expanses of empty soil between plants.

Miniatures are an unexpected pleasure in hanging baskets and window boxes, and they work well in both. A pot with a miniature can be a summer-long centerpiece on an outdoor dining table. Miniature roses do well in strawberry pots. On top of a stone wall where they can be viewed at eye level is another good spot for them. To keep a miniature rose small in a 6- to 8-inch pot (such as the kind that many are purchased in), prune the roots yearly when you prune the branches. Miniature roses can be cut and used in tiny arrangements, boutonnieres and corsages, and the best part is that the more blooms you cut, the more blooms the plant produces because cutting encourages growth.

MINIATURES FOR HANGING BASKETS

'Green Ice'
'Judy Fisher'
'Kathy'
'Lavender Jewel'
'Lavender Lace'
'Lemon Delight'
'Loveglo'
'Over the Rainbow'
'Red Cascade'
'Spring Song'

A mixture of miniature roses can easily be grown in half barrels.

There is nothing miniature about the heights the miniature climbing rose 'Red Cascade' can reach. The specimen pictured here reaches 15 feet high.

SPACING OF ROSES

To estimate the number of rosebushes needed for a garden, measure the garden's size in square feet. Depending on the type of rose and the climate in your area, the spacing of the bushes will vary. If, for example, you're planting hybrid Teas and the winter temperature in your area goes from 20° to 0° F. or below, the spacing should be between 24 and 30 inches. Where the growing season is longer, even year 'round in Zones 9 and 10, the bushes grow larger, so more space is needed between them.

A minimum spacing of 18 to 24 inches away from a building is necessary for all roses. Plan for air circulation between plants to help control powdery mildew. If you plant closer than the recommended spacing, the roses must be pruned to keep them within their allotted space. Space roses as follows:

Tree Roses—3 to 5 feet
Miniature Roses—12 to 18 inches
Climbing Roses—4 to 5 feet
Hybrid Teas—2 to 3 feet
Shrub Roses—3 to 5 feet

To estimate the number of rose bushes required:

Distance Apart	*Divide the Square Feet in the Bed by*
18 inches	2
24 inches	4
30 inches	7
36 inches	10
42 inches	12
48 inches	15

Perfume of Roses

Attar-of-roses, a yellow-green oil extracted from the petals of the most fragrant damask roses, is used in making perfume. It is a volatile oil concentrated in the cells at the base of the petals just before the rose opens. The roses must be picked at the first light of dawn because by noon 30 percent of the oil is lost to evaporation, and 70 to 80 percent is lost by 4 P.M. The picking of the petals is finished before 10 A.M., and they are processed the same day. It takes a ton and a half of fresh-plucked rose petals to produce a pound of attar-of-roses. The price of a pound of attar-of-roses fluctuates between two and three times the price of a pound of gold. It's no wonder the most expensive perfume in the world is Joy, a blend of roses and jasmine. Not everyone can afford rose perfume, but anyone with a garden can grow a fragrant rose that will willingly and wantonly share its scent.

THE ROSE PLANTING AND GROWING GUIDE

PLANTING ROSES

Controversy abounds on the subject of growing roses well. I've seldom met two rosarians who agreed on the methods of growing roses or even on which roses to grow. For every rule there is an exception—it's similar to the rearing of children. Everyone argues they need good nutrition, discipline and sunshine, but every parent's methods differ. Rosarians agree that roses are voracious eaters, heavy drinkers and sun worshippers, preferring the most fertile, well-drained lands, until it is pointed out that some roses (wild roses, species roses and shrub roses) fend for themselves even in poor soil and a few even in shady places (see page 89). Hotly debated topics include the control of insects and diseases.

The amazing truth is that gardeners are right in what they do in their own garden, assuming whatever they do works for them. Where they go wrong is in thinking it will work for someone else under different conditions. The brambles of advice become untangled as you prune away the excess with common sense. If you make foolish mistakes, you are in the best of company. It has been said that every garden has its story; some have virtual novels. Every rosarian has his or her own tales of woe and of triumph. Unintentionally over the years, I have mis-treated numerous roses; some drowned, others starved, bringing painful and expensive lessons while I learned how to provide care and nutrition. Every gardener starting out could use an adviser, but every good gardener eventually learns more by making mistakes.

There are myriad local rose societies around the country; it is easy to locate and join one. Each club has rosarians willing and able to give advice that applies to your area of the country. One thing is sure: The more you read about roses, the more you'll be inspired to work in the garden, and the more you share your experiences with other gardeners, the faster the knowledge comes. The longer a person gardens, the more individual her or his methods. Rosarians seem the most individualistic of all gardeners. Old methods are shortened and new methods are adapted using ever-improved products. I have favorite methods, but I also try new things each year in pursuit of better roses.

Selecting the Site

In selecting a site there are four things to consider: the amount of sunshine, the soil's drainage, the air circulation and the roots of nearby trees and shrubs.

There is an extensive variety of roses available, with enough diversity to please anyone. Pictured here are 'Belle de Crecy', 'Pink Grootendorst', 'Mary Rose' and 'White Meidiland'.

All roses do better in sunshine. Five to six hours of sunshine is adequate, and the flower colors shouldn't fade. In a sunny area, roses produce more flowers faster. If given a choice, early morning sun is preferable to afternoon sun. Wet leaves from morning dew or early watering dry more quickly in morning sun and dry leaves are less prone to black spot, rust and mildew.

After too little sunshine, poor drainage is the rose's most serious enemy. Contrary to popular belief, most roses don't grow well in clay soil. I garden in soil that previously was a brick yard. Finer clay you couldn't find. After years of preparing the top 3 feet of soil by adding compost and peat moss as a bed for modern roses, I still had trouble with the clay below, which held water until it backed up and gave the hybrid Teas wet feet. Eventually I had to remove and replace the soil to a depth of 3 feet, and in addition, add drainage pipes to carry excess water away. It is pointless to try to grow beautiful roses without good drainage. Roses drown if their roots stand in water. As long as water drains through, a soil on the heavy side is best for roses.

Run a soil test. Dig a hole 18 inches deep (the depth of the roots of most mature rose bushes), fill it with water and wait to see how long it takes to empty. If water remains in the hole six hours later, it is necessary to improve the drainage before planting roses. Add agricultural gypsum to lighten clay soil and to break apart the soil particles for better drainage and leave space for oxygen. Gypsum adds calcium and sulphur to the soil, enhancing root growth as it improves drainage. Peat moss and compost should be added too to help absorb excess water.

Mounding the soil 8 to 10 inches higher and creating a raised bed will also measurably improve the drainage. In extremely wet areas it may be necessary to add a retaining wall of railroad ties or stone to raise the garden even higher or to bury drainage pipes 2 feet deep to remove the excess water to another part of the garden and prevent backup water from drowning the roses.

Design your beds so they are not too deep and awkward to work. Try to avoid having to step into the bed often as this compacts the soil, slowing the drainage and forcing out oxygen. If the back of the bed is next to a building or a fence, a path a foot and a half wide and covered with mulch can be left unplanted at the back for the gardener's work space and passageway. From the front of the garden this path won't be visible.

Avoid planting in low areas. Cold air is heavier than warm air and collects in the lowest areas. When stagnant, cold air creates a frost pocket, it can kill even hardy roses. The opposite—a high, windy area where winds, like a herd of horses, trample everything in their path—can be another problem. The winds will blow-dry the roses with hot air in the summer and damage frozen canes in winter, snapping them off. Windbreaks of hedges, fences and walls will be necessary to protect roses from damage caused by strong winds.

Although many old garden roses are able to fend for themselves, roots from trees or shrubs can be troublesome if they're too close to where most modern roses are planted. The competition is too much for all but the species, shrub and wild roses. Protect a modern rose's roots by placing a vertical shield of galvanized metal stripping, 18 to 24 inches wide (available from some nurseries and lumber yards) underground between the rose bushes and the tree or shrubs. Even aggressive perennials that grow to a depth of 18 inches can interfere with some modern roses, robbing them of nutrients, water and living space. Rarely is there a perfect site. By understanding your site before you plant and correcting any potential problems, you are well on your way to growing healthy roses. The next most important step is to select the roses that like the conditions you can't change.

Preparing the Rose Bed

A rose well planted is on its way to being well grown. Planting is not an area in which you take a short cut. Good soil preparation will make the difference between a healthy rose and a rose susceptible to disease. Most roses are voracious feeders and need enriched soil. A rose grown in poor, lean soil is unlikely to attain full beauty.

Before preparing a bed for roses or rejuvenating a rose bed, a soil test should be made. Check for pH, minerals and trace elements. PH testing kits and meters are available at nurseries and through garden catalogs. Ideally the pH should be between 6.0 and 6.8. It is important to check the pH in a rose garden several times a season. Acid rain in many parts of the country can lower the pH to unacceptable levels over a season. A soil too alkaline or too acid inhibits the plant's ability to use the nutrients in the soil. Five pounds of ground limestone per 100 square feet of garden will raise the pH one point. To lower from .5 to 1 point, add 3 pounds of iron sulfate or ½ pound of ground sulfur per 100 square feet of garden.

Over time adding both peat moss and compost will lower the pH. Keep in mind that anything added to the soil will not be an immediate fix but will take time to break down in the soil. Adding organic matter such as compost, leaf mulch and peat moss improves the tilth of the soil, holds air, attracts earthworms and creates an ideal condition for the bacteria necessary to break down the nutrients into a useable form for the plants. Prepare a rose garden ideally in the fall for spring planting or a few weeks or a month before the roses are added to allow the bed to settle, preventing large air pockets, and the nutrients to meld. Planting time for areas where winters are severe is in the spring; for areas with mild winters, spring or fall; and in warm climates in the winter.

Once it's prepared, don't step in the garden bed unnecessarily. Compacting the soil, especially when damp, forces the oxygen out of the air spaces. The roots of roses need oxygen to live.

Planting Roses

Bare-root roses are available through the mail and from nurseries early in the season. They are less expensive than potted roses, and easy to train so the roots grow out into the garden soil. Container-grown roses are easier to plant, but beware of rose bargains late in the planting season. Many times the roses have been in the pots too long. Their roots, ingrown and twisted, are unable to grow out into the soil in search of nutrients. Stunted roots produce stunted canes with few flowers.

I have written off a rose as a poor performer only to dig it up and discover it had failed to develop an adequate root system. Organic products, such as the water-soluble Roots, can prevent this from happening. After planting the rose, water with a solution of Roots every month according to the manufacturer's directions until the rose is well established.

A bare-root rose could also benefit from being potted first in a good sterile soil and placed in a shady spot for a month where it will not be distracted by the sun from setting good roots. Hybrid Tea roses and roses transplanted to a windswept spot find this a helpful step. Check bare-root roses to see if any of the roots are broken or damaged and, if

Where drainage is poor, a raised bed will provide the well-drained conditions roses need for abundant bloom. The edges of the raised bed may be decorated with mounds of sweet alyssum seeded in early spring.

they are, cut off the problem area. Cut back the dark areas at the end of the canes by a few inches and remove any damaged canes. If any canes are crisscrossing as they grow, cut one or both out so they won't rub together.

As soon as you receive a bare-root rose, totally submerge the entire plant in a bucket of warm water for a minimum of 24 hours to a maximum of 72 hours. Bare-root roses become dehydrated during shipping. Add a polymer to the water before planting to prevent transplant shock (see page 34). If the rose's roots are swished through a slush of water with polymers, the polymers will adhere to them. Once the bush is planted, polymers keep moisture readily available for the roots. If you can't plant the rose immediately after soaking, protect it from dehydration. Heel it into a temporary hole until you have time to plant it properly. The temporary hole can be shallow with the rose laid on its side and covered, canes and all, to keep them from sprouting until transplanted in their permanent home.

"Never plant a rose in soil where another rose has grown as it may contain soil-borne diseases," is another rosarians' chant. This is nearly impossible in small gardens. Wherever the rose is to be planted, it's best to prepare the hole well.

Dig individual holes for roses 24 inches deep and several inches wider than the circumference of the roots or root ball. The hole should be large enough for the planted rose to be surrounded on all sides by well-supplemented, nutritious soil. Depending on your type of soil and the amount of preparation previously done in the bed, add approximately ½ to equal amounts of a mix of compost, peat moss, and/or well-rotted manure to the soil removed from the hole. All three additives will improve the structure of the soil and, in addition, manure and compost add nutrients. At the very least, purchase dried cow manure and peat moss from a nursery. For bare-root roses, center the soil in the hole in an inverted cone shape. The old Native American custom of burying a fish head an inch or two below the plant's roots is a good practice. As it decays, the fish head will release nutrients, naturally helping the rose through its first season. The roots of roses grow out from the bud union, the place of the graft. The rose

is planted so the bud union sits on top of the cone of soil with the roots supported by the cone's sides. The roots must be spread out evenly and pointed downward. When the bud union is placed on the cone it should be above ground in southern climates, level with the ground where winters are mild and an inch or two lower in northern, colder areas. If a straight stick is placed across the hole it is easy to see where the bud union is in relation to the ground level. If the rose doesn't have a bud union, it is planted with the roots and 1 inch of the cane under ground. If the soil has been recently prepared and hasn't been allowed to settle, it will compact somewhat and more soil might have to be added later to assure the bud union is planted at the proper depth.

For a potted rose the hole and soil are prepared in the same way but without the cone-shaped pile of soil. The rose is removed from the pot and the roots are gently released from the soil to help them grow out into the new soil and not wind around into themselves. The roots, soil and all, are placed in the hole with the bud union at the level as described above.

Fill the hole with the remaining soil and firm it in place by gently tamping it down around the bush with your feet. Add a slow-release fertilizer, well-rotted manure and Epsom salts (see Fertilizer, page 39). Mound a rim of soil 6 to 8 inches high around the edge of the hole to protect the bud union from wind and to hold water. Water with a gentle trickle until the hole is full and

water starts to run down the sides. If planting early, when a chance of cold, harsh weather is still possible, mound the soil up around the canes to a height of 8 inches to warm the canes and protect them from drying winds until the weather warms and growth begins. Always water in new rose bushes at the time of planting.

Polymers

Polymers, granules or crystals that absorb many times their weight in water and nutrients and release them slowly, are very useful in the battle against drought. Their ability to absorb and hold water in the soil, slowing down evaporation and preventing nutrients from leaching away, means containers or garden beds with polymers don't need to be watered or fertilized as often. Depending on the soil, and where it is used, a polymer's life span can be from three to 10 years. It must be mixed evenly into the soil, the amount not exceeding what is recommended by the manufacturer.

Both potted roses and bare-root roses experience less transplant shock if their root balls or bare roots are dipped in a bucket of water to which polymer crystals or powder has been added. After the polymer has been allowed to sit in the water and expand into a slurry mixture (approximately 10 minutes), the rose's bare roots can be dipped and swished around in the mixture to help the granules adhere to the roots. When the rose is planted, the granules will hold moisture where it is needed.

PRUNING

Pruning is the kindest cut. Its purpose is to remove diseased, damaged and dead wood, to shape the bush and to encourage new growth with lots of flowers. Prune to remove dead wood, to keep the rose healthy, to force the rose to grow stronger canes, and to keep the shrub within bounds. The flowers are produced at the top of the bush. Do you want roses to look up to, at eye level, or beneath you?

The canes continue to grow throughout the frostfree season in each area of the country. Faster growth comes earlier in the season, growing several feet or more depending on the type of bush. I prefer bigger, bushier roses than standard recommendations—no wimpy dwarf bushes for me. My eight-year-old pair of 'Queen Elizabeth' roses are 8 feet tall, a foot for each year. They are pruned yearly to remove dead canes and lower them by half, but the older, strong canes have not been removed. The top third of the slim upright bush is covered with roses. They rise at the two corners to anchor the garden. At their back and side are several shrubs of *Rosa* 'The Fairy' to hide their bare bottoms.

The body shapes and patterns of growth vary greatly with the type of rose. Roses aren't meant to all look alike, and they shouldn't all be pruned the same way. Look at each rose and consider its type and average height before visualizing the perfect shape for it. The healthiest canes show even coloration with many buds. The buds along the cane at this early stage are not flower buds but the beginnings of new leaves and canes located at nodes along each cane. They are pointing in the direction a new cane will grow.

In the fall in areas with below-freezing temperatures, only excessively long canes should be pruned back. Keep the canes the same height as the majority of stems to create a sturdier bush for protection from wind, snow and ice damage. The fewer open cuts on a rosebush going into winter, the better. Any open cuts are places for insects or fungus to creep in and make canes more susceptible to winter-kill. Climbers, old roses and shrub roses may not need to be touched until spring, and even then they need only to have the dead, damaged branches and excessively long canes removed.

The place the rose is planted will in part dictate pruning requirements. For example, a hedge of 'The Fairy' growing along a solid fence might require the posterior pruned somewhat flat to allow air circulation between the fence and the roses. This also encourages the rose to send more branches forward and allows air to circulate between the fence and the bush.

Some ramblers and climbers grow 20 to 30 feet and beyond, while others grow 8 to 12 feet. To keep a larger one in bounds it may need to be pruned back. Usually climbers are too high and too hard to reach, and Mother Nature takes over and gives them the ability to care for themselves. If the rambler or climber blooms only once a season, it can be pruned where necessary immediately after it blooms. Check to see that new shoots are coming from its base

Basics of Pruning

While the amount of pruning and the shape of the bush vary with the particular variety, the basics for pruning all roses are the same:

1. Cut each cane on a 45-degree angle, slanting downward to the inside of the bush, 1/4 inch above an outward-facing leaf bud, to encourage that bud to grow. If you can't find an outward-facing bud, cut above a node and a bud will be encouraged to grow.

2. Cut out all dead branches and, on hybrid Tea roses, any canes that are thinner than a pencil. These are too weak to be productive.

3. Cut out branches that cross each other or are too dense, as they can prevent air circulation in the center of the bush.

4. Cut out any winter-killed tissue, the dark areas at the end of some canes. All the dead area has been cut out when the healthy white pith inside the cane can be seen.

5. Look for signs of borers. A dark spot in the center of the end of the cane shows a borer has entered. Cut the cane to below the borer, if possible where the pith is white. At times a cane might have to be cut flush with the bud union, although rarely does the borer go this far (see Pithborers, page 84). Some rosarians seal each cut cane with a dab of Elmer's white glue to help prevent boring insects from re-entering the cane.

6. Discard any pruned canes, but don't add them to the compost heap as they may carry disease.

7. In late fall, cut back any excessively long stems to prevent damage by winter storms.

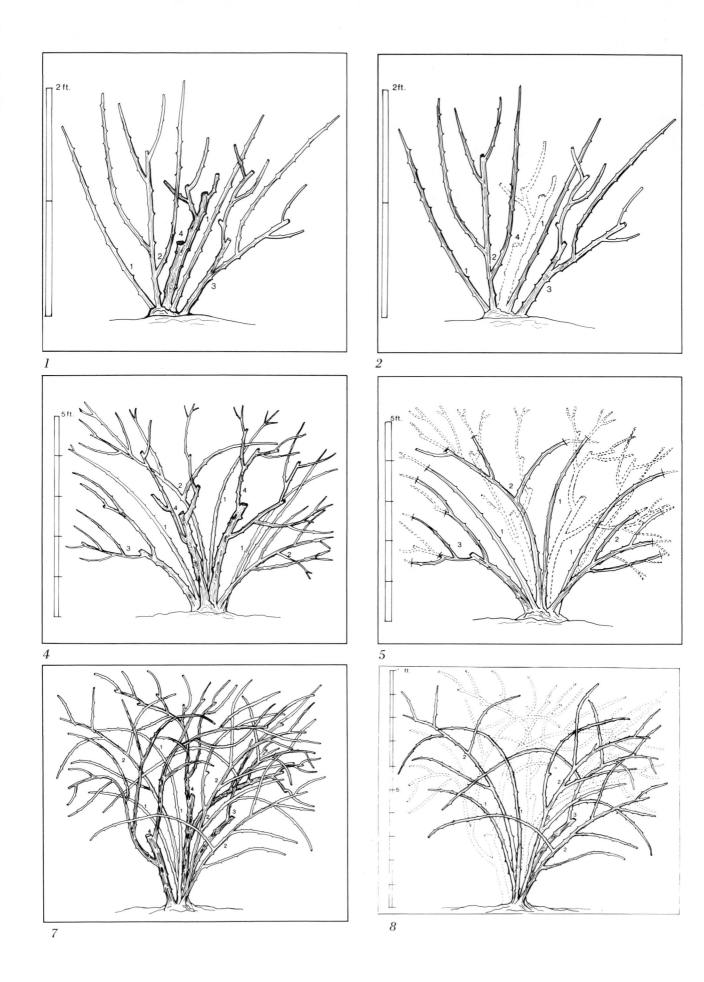

1

2

4

5

7

8

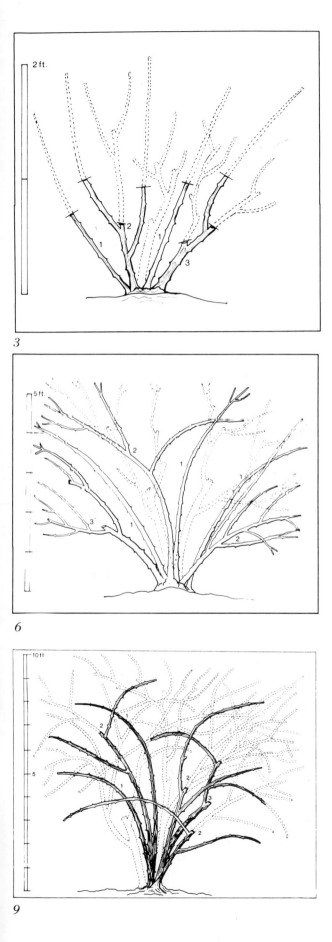

3

6

9

How to prune a bush rose, such as hybrid tea, floribunda and grandiflora types.

1) Unpruned bush rose.

2) Remove dead, dying and diseased wood. Remove stems more than 2 or 3 years old, and shorten others back to young branches, preferably one-year canes.

3) Shorten one-year canes to shape the plant and encourage growth from lower buds for compactness.

4) Unpruned shrub rose.

5) Remove dead, dying and diseased wood. Remove the oldest, most woody stems, usually those more than 3 years old. Less vigorous plants may require keeping more of their older wood. Shorten other stems back to young offshoots to remove congested, least vigorous twiggy branches.

6) Shorten remaining one-year growth by as much as a third to shape the plant and make it more compact. Twiggy side growth can be shortened to two or three buds to increase their vigor. If shoots are not shortened, the shrub will have a leggy appearance. The fewer buds there are per branch, the larger the flowers, but there will be fewer of them.

7) Unpruned climbing rose.

8) Remove dead, dying and diseased wood. Remove the oldest, most woody stems, usually those more than 3 years old. Less vigorous plants may require older wood to remain. Shorten others back to young offshoots to remove congested, least vigorous twiggy branches. The stems may become detached during pruning, but will probably need to be rearranged to fill in gaps. Tie all branches to support them, using soft string; move them to fill spaces as necessary.

9) Shorten one-year canes to achieve a good distribution of buds over the plant. Shorten side branches, depending upon their vigor, leaving only one or two buds on the weaker ones. Young vigorous canes can be left quite long. The fewer buds per branch, the larger the flowers, but there will be fewer of them.

before pruning too much. The shorter climbers should be pruned to force the main canes to grow up and out the sides, arching into a fan shape against the wall. With arched branches, more of the cane is exposed to the sun, encouraging more flowers to form at each node. Each spring the lateral branches growing off the main canes should be pruned back to ⅓ their length. If the climber or rambler is trained to grow over an arch or trellis, thin out any dead canes. Keep the canes from becoming too dense and tangled.

Conventional wisdom for hybrid Teas and grandifloras is to prune out all but two to four strong canes. Floribundas are traditionally pruned back to ⅓ the length of the cane to encourage outward-facing buds and a fuller figure. Hybrid Teas are usually pruned to be no higher than 6 to 10 inches each spring. Once they are pruned hard and new growth begins, they are fed often, more than any other plant or shrub. One of the best-cared-for rose gardens I know, Robert Sabin's in New York, gets pruned back only to good wood; all the strong canes are left. In early

summer his hybrid Teas (he has more than 850) are 4 feet high, with many more blooms than one would find on severely pruned bushes. The spring pruning height is determined by the amount of winter damage. Robert believes the previous year's growth is a victory of sorts, and that "severe pruning puts the roses in harm's way." The plants are too stressed when cut lower than they need be and full bushes hide the mulched soil with blooms at arm's level for easy enjoyment and picking. Fewer bushes are needed as each bush covers a larger area. In order to avoid being forced by winter's ravages to severely prune your rose, Robert recommends three guidelines. First, roses must be properly maintained throughout the growing season to prevent defoliation from summer blackspot. A defoliated rosebush is a weakened rose easily damaged in winter. Second, a heavy watering after a black (hard) frost and before the ground freezes prevents the bush from becoming dehydrated. And, lastly, harden the canes and prepare them for winter with a potassium feast (see Winter Protection, below).

Many shrub and species roses can bloom and live long lives without pruning. Pruning large, elderly shrubs can be a painful and difficult job. I usually do it every few years and with protective gear: leather gloves, heavy jacket, heavy socks, tough denim pants. Many dead canes are in the center and bottom of the bush and as most stems arch out, there is usually a small crawl space under the bush to reach in and prune the stems from the bottom. It is difficult to prune inside the bush while standing or reaching from the top. I've never found time to prune the hedge of rugosas on the beach and rarely is a dead cane visible after the shrub has leafed out. If it is, it is a simple matter to cut it off.

Suckers are shoots or new canes that grow up from the roots of a rose. The sucker is undesirable on grafted roses because it will bear the flower of the roots, instead of the more desirable grafted, budded rose blooming on top. Cut any suckers off as soon as they are spotted. They will have the vigor of the roots and eventually, if left on, will weaken and kill the budded rose.

WINTER PROTECTION

Rosa moschata, the musk rose, blooms once a season with a wonderful fruity fragrance.

Winter protection prevents the ground from quickly freezing and thawing during abrupt changes in weather. Roses can be damaged or killed by sudden heavy frost, especially during a period of growth. It is better for the rose to be dormant throughout winter, not to awaken on an unusually warm

January and be slapped in the face with a heavy frost. Don't add your winter protection too soon. If you do, the increased warmth encourages the bush to grow, only to be damaged later by sudden temperature drops. Continue to water roses sparingly even after frost. Going into winter, they need moisture.

Potassium is an important mineral for sturdy stems and foliage. Weekly feeds of a gallon of liquid potassium (1 tablespoon of muriate of potash, 0-0-62, dissolved in 3 gallons of water) per bush or a granulated feeding of potash-magnesium (0-0-22) during the six weeks before the bushes go dormant will give the bushes an additional boost for winter, extending their hardiness into another hardiness zone, perhaps two. Excess potassium, when available in greater amounts than nitrogen and phosphorous, is known as the "potassium feast." It will block the growth-promoting effects of nitrogen and phosphorus, hardening the canes in time for winter. Don't feed them nitrogen. Nitrogen speeds growth rather than letting the roses go into dormancy. Nitrogen and other nutrients can be added to the soil after frost, immediately before the winter protection is added, so they will be slowly dissolved over the winter as rain and snow leach through the soil, delivering the nutri-

ents down to the roots. When the roses awaken in the spring, they will have all the necessary food ready for their use. Add ½ cup of Epsom salts, 2 to 3 inches of well-rotted manure and a sprinkling of lime around the base of each rose bush. A protective organic mulch piled on top will enrich the soil with nutrients as it decomposes and improve the soil's structure and moisture-holding properties. Well-rotted manure and shredded oak leaves are best if available. Otherwise, any shredded leaves, compost or soil mixed with peat moss and dried cow manure (bagged and sold in most nurseries) works fine.

Where winters are mild, a 3- to 4-inch layer of mulch will be enough, but in colder areas it

must be deeper. Far north it is necessary to tie the canes together with string and bring in more soil, mixed with well-rotted manure, to pile to a depth of a foot or more around the canes. For added protection, leaves and a burlap blanket can completely cover the tops of the canes. In windy areas a wind break of burlap secured onto 5-foot poles will help protect the bushes. In spring, be careful not to damage any emerging new shoots near the base of the rose bush when the mulch is pulled back from the bush and spread evenly around. Only in the most northern gardens, where more mulch is needed, will any excess mulch have to be removed from the area.

A BALANCED DIET OF NATURAL FERTILIZERS

A balanced diet for roses includes the "big three"—nitrogen, phosphorus and potassium—as well as the secondary elements of calcium, magnesium and sulfur. Other trace elements—boron, nickel, chlorine, copper, iron, manganese, molybdenum and zinc—round out the diet.

NITROGEN is essential for plant growth, but when in excess it forces lush but weak growth and few flowers. A nitrogen deficiency dwarfs a plant and the older leaves turn yellow, then brown.

PHOSPHORUS promotes stiff stems and is necessary for flowering and seed formation. A dwarf plant with dark, dull green foliage and often a pur-

ple leaf stem is a sign of phosphorus deficiency.

POTASSIUM, or *POTASH*, as it is more commonly called, is an important catalyst for photosynthesis, essential for starch formation and the movement of sugar in plant and seed formation. It also promotes stiff stems and is essential for good roots. A potash deficiency can be detected when the lower foliage turns yellow. Several feedings of potassium six weeks before the roses go dormant for the winter increases their hardiness by providing stronger, harder canes and healthier roots.

When planting roses it is best to add organic fertilizers rather than a concentrated chemical fertilizer. Organic fer-

tilizers break down, slowly releasing their nutrients into the soil; chemical fertilizers encourage quick, weak growth of foliage. Later, when foliage is growing well after spring pruning, add a slow-release fertilizer or a soluble fertilizer. Old roses that bloom once a season don't want to be fertilized through the season. Continue fertilizing everblooming varieties monthly until two months before they go dormant. They will gradually slow their growth and not be snapped by a black frost while in full growth.

EPSOM SALTS contain magnesium sulfate, an important mineral for roses. A lack of magnesium causes foliar problems, fewer blooms and may even dwarf the plant. A half

cup of Epsom salts spread at the base of each rose bush in late fall and early spring will provide all the magnesium that is needed. The name Epsom salts comes from the original preparation, wherein the salts were obtained by boiling down the mineral waters at Epsom, England. Today the product is produced from seawater.

HORSE MANURE, while too rich in nitrogen for many plants, is perfect for roses. Not only does it feed the roses but it helps to improve the soil's texture and retention of moisture and air. The Long Island Rose Society recommends applying horse manure when it is only a week old and the nitrogen content is highest. This is fine in early spring, a few months before the roses bloom, but later in the year well-rotted, odorless manure is better and doesn't interfere with the rose's perfume.

LEAF MULCH and/or compost provides a more balanced diet of primary and trace elements than chemical fertilizers. It also improves the soil's structure while providing warmth to protect the roses in cold climates from harsh winter weather. Oak leaves, if readily available, are the best choice because they don't mat. Beware of maple and poplar leaves because, when used unshredded, they mat and prevent air and water from reaching the soil.

ALFALFA PELLETS or **MEAL**, spread at the base of each rose, ½ cup per bush, promotes greener, healthier leaves. It doesn't induce flushes of weak green growth but rather makes nutrients available naturally. Alfalfa pellets and meal also include many of the trace elements needed for a well-balanced diet.

BONE MEAL is approximately 4 percent nitrogen, 10 to 20 percent phosphorus, and .2 percent potash. If sprinkled in the planting hole before the roses are set in, it will be available for the rose's roots; sprinkled on top of the soil it will simply stay there and not be carried down to the roots.

FISH EMULSION contains the basic three nutrients, nitrogen, phosphorus and potash. It can be added to the soil or dissolved in water and sprayed on the leaves as a foliar feed during the growing season. Follow the manufacturer's directions.

SUL-PO-MAG or **LANGBENITE** is a natural mineral product imported from Canada and a good source of potassium. It contains approximately 22 percent potassium, 11 percent magnesium and assorted trace elements.

CHEMICAL FERTILIZERS break down quickly and the nitrogen leaches into the soil to pollute our water. Earthworms, the capable creatures who help do our tilling, can't live in a soil with chemical fertilizers. If you feel you need more nutrients for your plants than organic fertilizers provide, use only a slow-release fertilizer; it will break down slowly, staying in the top portion of the soil, where your plants can use it.

A FOLIAR FEED or soluble fertilizer such as Rapid-Gro 15-30-15, mixed according to the manufacturer's directions and sprayed at weekly intervals directly on the foliage, is extremely efficient as it is absorbed directly through the leaves and is immediately available to the plant.

COMPOSTING

A rose garden, like any other garden, is only as good as its soil. Composting for yearly replenishing of the nutrients in the soil is the single most important step a gardener can take toward building a beautiful garden. Without nutrients plants cannot continue to grow. Nature, however, makes it easy, and all the gardener needs do is follow her lead. A simple pile of leaves left behind the garage to decompose is perfectly adequate compost. The leaves will break down over the year into a fine, black humus that can be shoveled onto the garden bed each fall. Nutrients in the compost will be carried through the soil to the plant's roots by rainwater and will be readily available in the spring when needed by the roses.

Once you see the results of adding compost to your garden, you will not be willing to wait a year for the leaves to break down. There are almost as many different methods of composting as there are gardeners. The purpose of all the different methods is to speed up nature's decomposition. A pile left standing behind the garage to decompose on its own is the slowest method of producing compost. If leaves are layered in a compost bin alternately with an inch of soil, a sprinkling of ground limestone, a layer of horse or cow manure (to provide nitrogen) and watered thoroughly, the many organisms in the soil will help the leaves break down faster. Composting can be further speeded up if the pile is turned over with a shovel every week or two. Ready-made compost bins are designed to hold in heat, which speeds the process even more.

My preference is to rake leaves in the fall and shred them on the spot, returning them directly to the rose garden. Shredded leaves break down more quickly than whole ones. Shredded leaves are attractive as a mulch, give the roses winter protection and bring them nutrients in the spring. This eliminates the steps of bagging and moving the leaves, then carrying them back to the garden as compost in the summer. I do keep a compost pile for garden clean-up that is filled with excess leaves, vegetable peelings, grass clippings and other material gathered over the entire year, not just in the fall.

MULCH

An organic mulch, a minimum of 2 inches thick, conserves moisture, moderates the soil temperature, reduces the spread of fungus spores and discourages weeds. By covering the soil, it insulates it from the burning rays of the sun, keeping soil temperatures more even and slowing evaporation. Organic mulch made from shredded leaves, shredded pine bark, salt hay, well-rotted manure or peat moss mixed in equal parts with soil more than doubles the amount of water the soil can absorb. All roses, even roses planted in flower beds or mixed borders, can benefit from mulch under their branches and at their bases. Caution: Peat moss alone placed on top of the soil will form a hard, dry, impenetrable crust off which water will roll and not be absorbed.

WATERING

How you water and how much you water are important factors in growing roses. If you're using chemical fertilizers, water is necessary for them to dissolve for plant use. Water also moves nutrients from manures and other organic fertilizers placed on top of the soil to the plant's roots. The roses need water in their tissues, stems, petals and foliage.

What to put in the compost pile—	What not to put in the compost pile:
Remember that the smaller the pieces are, the faster they will decompose:	*cooked food* *weeds with seed pods* *any sawdust or shavings from treated wood (contains arsenic)*
shredded or whole fall leaves (first drag a lawn mower back and forth over leaves, or use a leaf shredder) *shredded bark (you'll need a wood chipper for this)* *shredded twigs* *fresh vegetable and fruit peelings* *grass cuttings* *tea leaves* *coffee grounds* *well-rotted horse or cow manure* *eggshells* *cut flowers* *pine needles*	*raw fish and animal remains (good compost, but they attract mice and other small animals)* *diseased plants (the disease will spread)* *any plant materials that have been treated with a herbicide or pesticide within the past three weeks*

Roses in the heat of summer need an inch of water every two or three days. If roses don't get enough water they become stressed and are easy victims for pests and disease. Roses love a morning shower followed by a sunny day. Water left for more than six hours on the leaves can spread black spot and mildew. Low sprinklers spraying water only 6 inches high, soaker hoses, drip systems and underground porous piping are the best methods of watering because they all keep the water off the roses' foliage and deliver water to where it is most effective, wasting little to evaporation or runoff. An underground porous pipe, buried 8 inches deep, will deliver water right to the roots while keeping the soil surface dry and discouraging weed seeds from sprouting. Water thoroughly so water penetrates the soil to a depth of 8 inches at each application. Proper watering can take several hours, depending on the delivery capacity of your equipment.

PROPAGATING ROSES

Cuttings

Many roses can be propagated from cuttings, a method similar to propagating perennials. In areas with a long, frostfree growing season, cuttings can be taken year 'round. In Zones 7 and lower, successful cuttings need to be propagated early in the rose season. Always try a few from the same bush to help ensure success. Look for a "perfect bloom" on a strong, healthy stem originating low on the bush and including several bud eyes. This is the stem you want to clone. The time to cut is when the bloom is ready to shatter. Cut a 10- to 12-inch stem and then take your 6-inch cutting from the midsection, the bottom cut square across just beneath a node (joint) and the top cut at a slant ¼ inch above the bud. Cut off all but the top two 5-leaflet leaves; this will help prevent wilting and promote rooting. If more leaves are left, it is harder for the stem to stay alive because the leaves zap the stem's energy. If you've taken the cutting from a friend's garden and won't be going home for a few days, or if it isn't possible to root the cutting immediately, wrap the ends in wet paper towels sealed in a plastic bag or place the cutting in water.

When ready to plant, dip the end of the stem into a rooting hormone. A rooting hormone stimulates root growth. Plant the stem 3 inches deep in a rooting soil, light enough for good drainage but heavy enough to stand the stem upright. The rooting soil should be moist, not soggy, consisting of coarse building sand, vermiculite or a mixture of peat moss and sand, or ⅓ perlite mixed with good potting soil. Perfect conditions for rooting cuttings are a humid atmosphere, good light without exposure to direct sun and moist soil. A 6-inch-diameter pot will hold six cuttings for the first two months of growth. Make a hole in the rooting medium with a pencil. This hole should be wider than the cutting stem, so the stem won't be damaged when placed in the hole. Stand the stem in the hole and gently firm the planting medium around the stem. When propagating new roses from cuttings it is safest to set up a misting tent complete with a timer, available at nurseries. An alternative is to set a cold frame on the north side of a wall. Homemade individual cold frames can be made from mason jars, ½-gallon plastic milk containers with their necks opened, and even plastic bags inverted over individual cuttings. Rooting is promoted by warmth and moisture, particularly bottom heat. Place the pot in a warm (70° to 80° F.) spot, out of direct sunlight. Check regularly to see that the atmosphere around the stems is not too dry or too moist. Droplets of water inside a misting tent or cold frame indicate too much moisture and promote mildew. If droplets form, vent the pot so air can circulate. When new growth appears, usually in six to eight weeks, remove the cover. Transplant each cutting into its own pot to grow on for another three weeks before planting into the garden. A cutting will probably flower in three or four months.

A careful and dedicated gardener can start cuttings without any cover, but it is necessary to keep a watchful eye. Check the soil at least once a day to see if it needs moistening, more often in hot weather. If practical, place it in a spot you pass frequently so you won't forget to water.

Some modern roses are protected by plant patents and can't be propagated without breaking the law, even for private enjoyment. Older roses and roses not protected by patents may be propagated. Roses grafted onto another's root stock are probably not good candidates for root cuttings because they will lack the vigor when grown on their own roots. However, some are good candidates. Rose growers often use grafted stock because roses can be propagated faster if grafted onto other roots. I have, however, seen hybrid Tea roses grown on their own roots that grew beautifully.

Layering

In layering, a portion of a stem is induced to root while the stem is still connected to and nourished by the mother plant. This requires tender stems with the flexibility to arch to the ground to allow a few inches of the stem, approximately a foot from the end, to be buried in a 6- or 7-inch-deep hole. The part of the stem to be buried should be just above a bud eye, and the thin outer layer should be carefully scraped off. The pith underneath is then coated with rooting hormone and buried. The portion of the stem that has been scraped is where the roots of the new rose will grow. The hole is filled with a mixture of sand and vermiculite or sand and peat moss. It is usually necessary to weight the stem to hold it down. Layering takes a year or longer before the roots are strong enough for the plant to be severed from the mother plant and moved to its new location.

Runners

A runner is an underground root that sends up a new stem (sucker) a short distance from the main canes. Many of the old roses increase readily by runners. In a small garden runners can become a nuisance, but on a beach, in the case of rugosas, or on a hillside to stop erosion, runners can be welcome. A runner can't be severed and grown immediately on its own; it needs a little help from the gardener when being transplanted. Carefully dig the new cane and its roots, trying not to damage any roots. Sever the underground runner and remove the new rose. Soak the roots in Roots to help stimulate root growth. Plant it in a pot with a good planting medium such as Pro-mix and place it in a shady spot. It is important to encourage more roots to help the bush live on its own. If placed in the sun the bush will spend too much energy trying to flower and grow on top rather than establishing healthy roots. After a month the new bush can be planted in a permanent place in the garden.

DEADHEADING ROSES

Deadheading is the removal of dead blossoms. Depending on the variety of rose, deadheading can make a big difference. Dead flowers with petals that cling as they brown rather than fall to the ground can be unsightly, distracting from the beauty of the flowers still blooming. Cut the dead flower off the flower stalk just below the first true leaves. As winter approaches it is healthier for the roses to allow hips to form instead of forcing the rose to continue flowering. The formation of seed prepares the rose for winter and increases its hardiness. Some roses are "self-cleaning," the petals falling on their own. Roses that bloom once and form ornamental hips shouldn't have their flowers removed. The decorative hips that form can be a feast for the birds as well as a beautiful sight for the gardener.

PRACTICAL PRACTICES WITH CLIMBERS

Climbers don't really climb, at least not the way vines do, with clinging tendrils, twining supple stems or aerial roots to pull them up. What sets roses apart is their long awkward canes. Most climbing and rambler roses sprawl, arch, creep and scramble over the ground,

At Planting Fields Arboretum, on Long Island, an old rose of unknown origin climbs metal arches over a walkway through the perennial garden.

stretching out with long stems. None will do exactly what you wish. All are like wayward children, needing guidance. Successful climbers need to be watched during periods of quick growth so you see what they want to do and then learn to work with them. To grow up, roses must be secured to latticework, a pillar, a fence, a trellis, an arch, a porch or the side of a building. Because they travel straight up, the feet of climbing roses are exposed to the drying sun. They need shade on their roots, which is why climbing roses do well as a backdrop to a flower border. The bordering flowers shade their roots, and the combined bloom at various heights adds to the beauty of the planting. Depending on the variety, canes grow from 6 feet to more than 60 feet.

I have seen roses climbing on many ingenious homemade supports. Bob Titus, a former director of Planting Fields Arboretum, Oyster Bay, New York, made arches from the metal rods used as reinforcement in concrete. These are available in 20-foot lengths, cost under ten dollars and are easily bent. If the metal is threaded through an old green garden hose its color blends with the foliage and the rod won't rust. The ends of the arch are anchored in larger metal pipe sunk 18 inches into the ground. When densely covered with roses the arch is invisible. Many formal gardens have pillars with chains loosely draped between them for the roses to grow along. At Old Westbury Gardens on Long Island the chains are waist-high at the back of the garden, where they provide a finishing edge and stop the eye from wandering onto the lawn beyond. The Brooklyn Botanic Garden uses similar supports, but with the chains higher on the pillars; there the roses are strung overhead.

Ready-made arbors, arches, trellises and gazebos are available in rustic and formal designs and in a variety of woods and metal. Usually plastic trellises are too flimsy. The trick with an arbor is to make sure it is secure in the ground. Select one that is sturdy and bury the bottom poles 18 inches in the ground for a strong support. A permanent structure can be set in cement. Wooden trellises can be placed to create a shady spot where you can sit and rest or enjoy outside dining. At the beginning or end of a walk, a trellis says welcome. For growing a pillar rose, metal supports with notches to hold chicken wire fencing come in different heights, are extremely sturdy and can be placed singly.

One of the simplest methods to train a climber is to secure horizontal pairs of eye hooks 3 feet apart into a wall at 1-foot increments and reaching up the wall. Tightly stretch wire between the hooks. As the rose grows higher, additional hooks and wires can be added. Loosely tie the canes to the structure using a soft or elastic material such as string, foam-covered wire or strips of fabric. Never tie the canes with wire, which will cut through them when they are bent and pushed about by the wind. Train young canes early to grow in the direction you wish. Gently bend canes into a fan shape against a building, and direct individual canes to climb around a window, spiral up a pillar or clamber up and over an arch or gazebo. Prune out canes growing in the wrong direction to encourage growth in the right direction. Vigilantly watch growth early in the spring and summer. Growth slows with higher temperatures and revives in the cool fall.

At Old Westbury Gardens, this rustic, wooden trellis is covered with 'American Pillar' roses.

GROWING ROSES IN CONTAINERS

Many roses grow well in containers, where they have the advantage of being mobile and can add decoration wherever they are wanted.

In northern areas, tender roses can be grown in pots and moved indoors for winter. In a garden where nearby roots of trees or shrubs might choke them, containers of roses can be buried. The pot will protect the rose from any invasion.

Purchased potting soil will give container-grown roses a head start, eliminating the potential setbacks of weed seed, soil-borne diseases and soil-borne insects. Most potting soils include nutrients important for the first month or more of growth. Roses in containers need regular liquid fertilizing to look their best.

A 5-gallon pot is large enough to house a hybrid Tea or a floribunda, but a 7- to 10-gallon container is better, allowing the plant more room to wiggle its toes. Larger containers hold more water and nutrients and will not dry out so quickly. However, during the high heat of summer, any pot may need daily watering. Be sure there is a drainage hole in the bottom of the pot to prevent overwatering. This is especially important for pots placed where rain water can reach them.

Containers dry out more quickly than gardens because the sun bakes the containers on their sides as well as their tops. There are ways to slow the drying process. One of the best is to add polymers to the soil before planting (see page 34). Another is to double-pot the rose. To double-pot, place the potted rose inside a larger pot, at least 4 inches larger in diameter and 2 inches taller. Pack the area between the pots with peat moss. Keep the peat moss wet. It will absorb heat and deflect it from the soil around the rose. If the inside pot is terra cotta, some of the moisture held by the peat moss can be absorbed into the soil through the side of the pot. Enough soil can be added to hide the rim of the inside pot. You can even put 8 inches of potting soil on top of the peat moss and seed or plant this area with an annual such as sweet alyssum, which will grow into a fragrant white ruffle in six to eight weeks and, by summer's end, spill over and down the sides of the pot. Another way to conceal double-potting is to cover it with florist's moss or Spanish moss, both of which act as mulch and slow down evaporation.

LONG-LASTING BOUQUETS OF ROSES

Pick roses early or late in the day (when they contain their most abundant nutrient and moisture supply), not under a wilting hot sun. Petals are plumper and more fragrant in the morning. Use sharp shears to cut the stems; a crushed stem won't take up water. Roses picked in bud (single blooms) or just beginning to open (semidouble or double roses) will last longer than full-blown roses. Full-blown roses are delicate and easily lose their petals. Some roses, if picked in tight bud, won't open but the buds are beautiful.

After you bring the roses inside, recut the stems on a slant to increase the surface of the stem exposed to the water. Many florists recut the stems under water to prevent air from entering the stem and clogging it. The stem's uptake of water is what keeps it firm and plump. If necessary, the foliage can be shined with a damp cloth or washed with warm soapy water. Any foliage below the water level should be stripped off because it will quickly decay under water. Place the roses in warm water (100° F.) and add floral conditioner to the water. Floral conditioners feed the roses while preventing bacteria from growing, doubling the life of your bouquet. If you don't use conditioners, the water should be changed daily as fungus and bacteria will cause an unpleasant odor as the flower stems decay. Let the roses sit in a dark, cool place for a few hours before arranging them. If time permits, place the roses in the refrigerator for a few hours or overnight. This will harden the stems and permit them to last longer in the vase.

Finally, for the smallest arrangements of all, there are lapel pins that hold the rose in water. Or, rose buds and roses just beginning to open will last out of water to wear for an evening.

On hot summer days, carrying a bucket of warm water to the garden for newly cut roses is the first step to conditioning them for longer vase life.

ROSE PORTRAITS

ROSE CLASSIFICATION

The genus *Rosa* is part of the larger family *Rosaceae*, which makes the rose a close relative of the strawberry, hawthorn, peach, almond, apple and apricot. Species roses have single, open, five-petaled flowers, similar in appearance and fragrance to apple and strawberry blossoms. Rose hips, the fruits of the rose, are richer in vitamin C than citrus fruits, apples and strawberries. Many rose hips, such as the large rugosa hips, can be used to make rose hip preserves.

There are more than eight thousand named rose varieties listed in the American Rose Registry, and more new introductions are added every year as breeders search for the ever-elusive, flawless bloom. Roses are classified by common characteristics as well as by use. In the Rose Portraits I have grouped them more by type or common characteristics, using Beverly Dobson and Peter Schneider's Combined Rose List as the authority (see page 91 for information on how to order). In the chapter *Designing with Roses*, they are mostly grouped by use, for example, tree roses, landscape roses, climbers and groundcover. The American Rose Registry lists more than 56 rose classifications. Over time, as new roses are bred with similar characteristics, new classes of roses have been formed. Grandiflora, the newest classification, was started in 1954 with the introduction of 'Queen Elizabeth'.

As new classifications are introduced, many older classes fall from grace, their offspring taking their place. Polyanthas were popular until the floribundas arrived, and the hybrid perpetu-als were more widely grown before the hybrid Teas. However, in each class many varieties deserve a second look and a place in today's garden. The hybrid perpetuals, with 90 percent of their bloom in early summer and only a light bloom in fall, are not as popular as hybrid Teas, which bloom modestly over the whole season. A hybrid perpetual in full bloom is a glorious sight, a show stealer, more so than most flowering shrubs that bloom only once a year. Classification of roses can be a bewildering maze and many experts contradict each other. For simplicity, I have loosely grouped roses into 16 classes.

It is difficult for rose lovers to limit the number of roses included in their gardens (or, in my case, in this book), and it is nearly impossible to prioritize classes of roses, so different, yet so much alike. New roses are introduced each year, and part of the fun is to find and grow some of them. You'll never in a lifetime get to know them all. I have tried to provide information on many popular roses that seem to be on everyone's list, as well as my favorites. The many lists throughout the book include roses less well known, and while not featured in the Rose Portraits—usually because of space limitations—they are nonetheless highly recommended. Acquaint yourself with the variety, versatility and broad spectrum of colors and color blends available. You can judge for yourself what makes a desirable rose. As your acquaintance with roses grows, your choices will reflect your taste. In the course of growing roses, most gardeners come across roses that for

'Ralph's Creeper' is a groundcover rose. The flowers are red in bud and when they first open. As they age, they change to various shades of pink. When in full bloom, the bush will have an assortment of roses in shades of pink and red at the same time.

whatever reason don't perform well in their garden and those should be "shovel pruned," as the saying goes, and taken out with the garbage.

As an additional guide, I have provided the official ARS rating, an average of the rating each rose received based on nationwide performance. Members rate roses on a scale from 1 to 10. Of course the beauty of the rose is in the eye of the beholder and many ARS members view a rose's beauty for its exhibition qualities, which may not match your criteria in growing roses. Roses perform variously in different geographical areas. If you're growing roses in California, luck is on your side; in Maine your choices are more limited. A rose may receive an ARS rating of 8.5 in one area but a 7.3 nationwide. Roses rated under 5.9 are considered not worth growing, but as with anything else you may find there are exceptions; many of these make excellent garden roses, even if they aren't roses of choice for competition. In some instances a rose is too new to have an ARS rating, or there is a lack of reports to establish the rating. Included for each entry are the rose's year of introduction, the name of its breeder (if known), awards it has won, its color classification, its fragrance and a physical description. It should be noted that the awards such as AARS are given to new introductions of roses, usually roses with characteristics valued for floriferousness and disease resistance. Rarely have climbers or shrub roses received awards. It goes without saying that older roses have never entered competitions.

ARS Rose Ratings (National)

10.0—Perfect
9.0–9.9—Outstanding
8.0–8.9—Excellent
7.0–7.9—Good
6.0–6.9—Fair
5.9 and lower—of questionable value

PLANT PORTRAIT KEY

Here is a guide to the symbols and terms we use throughout this section.

AARS: Only roses introduced since The All-American Rose Selections committee was formed in 1938 are eligible for this award. The abbreviation AARS followed by a year on a rose label or next to a rose's name identifies the year the rose was an All-American Rose Selection winner. The award was conceived to evaluate roses before they reached the marketplace, to help home gardeners select the roses best for them. Hybrid Teas, floribundas and grandifloras are the most common entries, but in recent years a few shrub roses have won. Entries are grown at 24 test gardens around the country representing a wide range of climates. They are evaluated for two years by experts who rate each rose's disease resistance, form, hardiness, flowers, and performance. Only about 4 percent of entries win an award. There are also 132 AARS rose trial show gardens at public gardens across the country where the public is invited to come and observe new roses growing a year before the roses are made available for sale.

Color Classifications are defined by the American Rose Society. Where I don't agree with the designated color, my interpretation follows in parentheses.

O—Once-a-year Bloomer: Roses that bloom once a season for a 3- to 4-week period. Many old roses are once-a-year bloomers.

R—Repeat Bloomer: Roses that bloom heavily in the spring, with perhaps a few blooms over the summer, and then a full, but not as heavy, bloom in the fall.

C—Continuous Bloomer: Many modern roses, such as the hybrid Teas, bloom modestly but continuously for many months.

Disease Resistance: This is difficult to rate as it depends so much on the rose's environment in addition to the variety of rose. Every rose responds better to optimum conditions, healthy soil, sun and abundant water. While all roses featured are recommended, roses with a reputation across the country for excellent disease resistance have been noted to guide the beginner.

Height: The height of the rose varies with the length of the growing season (a rose in California will be taller than the same variety in Maine), the richness of the soil, the amount of sun and rain, and the severity of the pruning. Average heights are listed only as a guide for planning the appropriate space in designing a garden and for comparison between one rose and another.

Hips: Outstanding ornamental hip display.

Blooms: Flower Description and Size:

single—4 to 7 petals in a single row

semidouble—12 to 24 petals in two rows

double—more than 25 overlapping petals in three or more rows

quartered—A quartered rose has so many petals tucked into a cup shape that the petals stand straight up flattened against each other. The petals form a scalloped arrangement that seems to divide the flower into four equal parts. The top of the flower is so flat that it appears to have been sliced off with a sharp knife.

The size of the flowers varies with the rose's diet and growing conditions. Most roses have larger flowers at the beginning of the blooming season.

Fragrance: Fragrance—if there is any—is described as slight, moderate or strong. Remember, fragrance may vary with the weather and the length of time the rose has been in bloom (see page 9).

Hardiness: All the roses listed are winter-hardy except where noted as tender. Hardiness varies with each rose and many of the modern roses will need winter protection in the coldest areas of the country.

Uses:

Beds—Good for planting in groups

Borders—Roses that easily combine with other plants

Containers—Good for growing in a container

Cutting—I have yet to meet a rose I wouldn't want to cut and bring indoors. Roses designated as good for cutting have long stems and are long-lasting in water.

Edging—Good for edging a garden

Groundcover—Roses that are wide growing and useful to cover a flat area or bank.

Hanging Basket—Roses with draping habits to hang over the edges of containers

Hedges—Good for use as a hedge

Houseplant—Good for growing under lights or in a sunny window indoors

OLD GARDEN ROSES AND ANTIQUE ROSES

The rise in popularity of old roses isn't the result of nostalgia alone. Their subtle, refined beauty, heady perfume and easy manners encourage even casual gardeners who haven't the time or inclination to fuss with and pamper the more uppity of the clan, the hybrid Tea. Old garden roses, or old-fashioned roses as they are sometimes called, are a loose grouping of direct descendants of roses cultivated and introduced before 1867 as well as some species hybrids. These roses are survivors. Many old roses are ignored for the sin of a short flowering season or, in some cases, small and unpretentious flowers. They bloom only once, but with reckless abandon and powerful fragrance! Giving their all, they produce in a three- to four-week period as many flowers as a modern rose does throughout the gardening season. They deserve to be as popular as other flowering shrubs such as lilac, azalea, rhododendron and forsythia. Needing only the simplest of care, they give much beauty in return.

In contrast to the upright canes of modern hybrids, many old roses choose to scramble along the ground, arch gracefully to tumble in fountainlike mounds or climb high into trees. Their colors are quiet, most soft and refined, so they easily complement their garden neighbors. Like other shrubs, they can be mixed in flower beds and need not be grown away from other plants. Their flowers may be simple and five-petaled, but many are semidouble or, often, cupped fully-double like the peony, or globular and romantic like the cabbage rose, the favorite model of many artists. These roses are valued for their mature, open blossoms, not their buds (the case with many modern roses), and they grow in beauty over the years. Old rose fragrances vary from the sweet to the musky; some of the most pleasing fragrances in the world of roses are found in this group.

Some newer hybrids of old varieties are included in the "old rose" classification and many of these are repeat bloomers. Old garden roses are extremely cold hardy, surviving in -30° to -40° F.; hybrid Teas won't. Old varieties aren't fussy about garden soil and don't need fertilizers or chemical sprays.

GALLICA ROSES (*ROSA GALLICA*, FRENCH ROSE)

Gallicas, the earliest recorded roses cultivated in Europe, probably originated in Eastern Europe or Asia Minor. Gallica varieties are fragrant with the scent known as the true old rose perfume. The most famous is *Rosa gallica officinalis* (the Apothecary's Rose), treasured for its purported medicinal properties and bright red color. It was indispensable in olden times for the making of a variety of medicines, and was first recorded growing during the Middle Ages in monastery gardens. It has a strong scent and, as its name implies, was used in the preparation of oils, syrups, salves and ointments to treat problems from melancholy to dysentery. Scientists today have not found any basis for the purported medical properties. The emperor Charlemagne had the Apothecary's Rose planted in the imperial garden.

The Apothecary's Rose is unusual in that it retains its fragrance when the petals are dried and powdered. Apothecary's Rose was brought to this country by the pilgrims and has naturalized in many areas of the country. Gallicas bloom only once, in midseason. Their flowers are flat in pink, purple and maroon, some with crimson shadings. They are low growing, rounded and neat, perfect for small gardens. As suckering roses, they spread by underground runners. Most Gallicas are winter hardy and more adaptable to poorer soils than other roses.

'Belle de Crécy'
Hybridizer, Date of Introduction: Before 1829
ARS Rating: 7.5
Color: Mauve and mauve blend
Blooms: 2½ to 3½ inches, quartered (100+ petals), O
Fragrance: Strong
Height: 4 to 5 feet
Uses: Beds, borders
Characteristics: 'Belle de Crécy' has deep pink, rounded, squat buds decorated with feathery sepals that open pink, tinged with violet. The velvety petals age to deep violet with rosy pink, small, incurving center petals that reveal a green button eye. While the color is unusual and distinctive, the bush to me always looks messy as the fading flowers hold their petals and take on a silvery gray cast before dying. It needs deadheading regularly and is best not used as a focal point. It is an arching shrub smothered with flowers in early summer. The foliage is gray-green and rough. The canes are covered with prickles.

'Charles de Mills'
Hybridizer, Date of Introduction: Roseraie de l'Hay, ca. 1800
ARS Rating: 8.5
Color: Mauve, mauve blend (red blend)
Blooms: 3 to 3½ inches, quartered (200 petals), O
Fragrance: Strong
Height: 5 feet
Uses: Beds, borders
Characteristics: 'Charles de Mills' is a labyrinth of deep crimson petals progressively tinged more purple and maroon as it ages into full bloom; buds are electric red. Each flower has a classic shape, quartered with a central button eye. 'Charles de Mills' always flaunts his fragrance. The

The velvety pink petals of 'Belle de Crécy' darken to a deep violet as the blossoms age.

flowers usually bloom in clusters of four on long, arching canes, 5 feet or longer. They bloom only in spring, but for a longer period than many old roses. 'Charles de Mills' is tolerant of partial shade. Of ancient and obscure origin, 'Charles de Mills' has few thorns and can be rooted from softwood cuttings. Eventually the shrub becomes as wide as it is high. Black spot may develop but is not debilitating.

'Complicata'

Hybridizer, Date of Introduction: —
ARS Rating: —
Color: Pink blend (medium pink)
Blooms: 4 to 5 inches, single (7 petals), O
Fragrance: Moderate
Height: 5 feet
Disease resistant
Hips
Uses: Beds, borders, climbing
Characteristics: 'Complicata' is a rose with a murky past. The only thing known for sure is that it has Gallica blood (its origin, date and parentage are unknown), so it is most often listed as a Gallica hybrid. The pointed buds open to vivid, rosy pink flowers with large white centers highlighted by pronounced golden stamens. The flowers are long-lasting, closing at night and opening with the sun; they fade to soft pink as they age. Blooms cover the shrub, flowering freely early in the season. 'Complicata' is a robust grower that adapts to poor soil and partial shade. Tied to a support to help it reach the lower branches of a

tree, its long canes can be made to grow 10 feet up, or it can be pruned to form a bush with arching branches, 5 feet tall. The light gray-green leaves are pointed with serrated edges. Colorful, round orange hips follow the flowers. Black spot occurs occasionally but is nothing to worry about. 'Complicata' can withstand winter temperatures to –25° F.

'Rosa Mundi' (*Rosa gallica versicolor*)

Hybridizer, Date of Introduction: ca. 1581
ARS Rating: 9.1
Color: Pink blend (white or near white with pink stripes)
Blooms: 2 to 3 inches, semi-double (18 to 24 petals), O
Fragrance: Moderate
Height: 3½ to 5 feet
Hips
Uses: Beds, borders
Characteristics: 'Rosa Mundi', a show-stopper when weighed down with flowers, is a most memorable rose—once seen, never forgotten. Each flower is broadly painted in streaks of carmine-pink across blush-white layers of petals, all loosely surrounding a fluff of golden stamen. It is a striped sport, an accident of nature, a chance offspring of the Apothecary's Rose. We know 'Rosa Mundi' as an old French rose cultivated prior to 1581. As the story goes, 'Rosa Mundi' was named after "Fair Rosamund," mistress of King Henry II, so this would seem to date the rose in the 12th century. 'Rosa Mundi' requires little fertilizer, growing in average soil. If over-fertilized, the stripes will be

less pronounced. Round, red hips appear in fall. It is a compact bush, hardy without protection to –15° F., and blooms only once in early summer. It gets black spot occasionally but the damage is usually minor.

'Charles de Mills' has more than 200 petals that become progressively more maroon in tint as they age.

'Complicata' is a robust grower that adapts to poor soil and partial shade.

The stripes of 'Rosa Mundi' are a beautiful accident of nature.

Damask Roses

Since the first century B.C., attar of roses has been made from Damask roses. Damask roses, descendants of gallicas, share the gallicas' intense fragrance. It is believed the Persians were the first to cultivate Damask roses. The crusaders are generally credited for bringing them to Europe. Damasks have lanky growth and are easily trained along fences and up pillars. The blossoms are semidouble or double (up to 60 petals) and generally bloom in long clusters of ready-made bouquets. Their foliage is mostly a gray-green with downy undersides. If the plants have hips, they are long and narrow. These are a hardy lot, surviving cold temperatures without protection in Zone 4.

'Mme Hardy' has a strong, sweet fragrance noticeable even from a distance.

'Mme Hardy'

Hybridizer, and Date of Introduction: 1832
ARS Rating: 8.8
Color: White or near white
Blooms: 2½ to 3½ inches, quartered (200+ petals), O
Fragrance: Strong
Height: 4 to 6 feet
Disease resistant
Uses: Cutting, beds, borders

Characteristics: One of the finest and purest white roses, 'Mme Hardy's' flowers glow against her dark green foliage. 'Mme Hardy' is a remarkable lady known for her beauty and loved for her strong, sweet fragrance with just a hint of lemon. Introduced as a cross between a Damask and an Alba or a Centifolia, the quartered flowers open cupped but flatten out on top as the outer petals reflex, swooning down to reveal green, button-eye centers (or pips). Occasionally, hints of a pink blush appear on some flowers. Blooms once a season but for more than a month. Prune down to a foot or two from the ground every three or four years, taking out the oldest canes as low as possible, and 'Mme Hardy' will reward you with a shapely figure. She is hardy to –30° F.

Bourbon Roses

Bourbons are fairly vigorous, compact shrubs usually 5 to 6 feet high, but the group also includes a few climbers. Combining the best qualities of old roses with the ability to repeat bloom, Bourbons' appearance depends on whether the predominant ancestral traits favor the China roses, as in 'La Reine Victoria', or the Damask, as in 'Souvenir de la Malmaison'. Most Bourbons have a fruity scent, frequently of apples, and a range of foliage colors from light to dark green tinted with copper, red or purple. They bloom on old wood, so don't prune the bush low in the spring.

'Zéphirine Drouhin' is an old climbing rose that will bloom in partial shade.

'Zéphirine Drouhin'

Hybridizer, Date of Introduction: Bizot, 1868
ARS Rating: 7.8
Color: Medium pink
Blooms: 2 to 4 inches, semidouble (15 to 20 petals), R, C
Fragrance: Moderate
Height: 8 to 15 feet
Uses: Pillar, climbing into a tree, trellis, wall
Characteristics: 'Zéphirine Drouhin' has a rich, sweet perfume and opens with semidouble, high-centered cerise-pink flowers on burgundy-colored canes. It is an almost thornless climber and has been known to bloom with only three hours of sun.

The new leaves are a copper-purple that age to dark green. Hardy to −10° F.

'Souvenir de la Malmaison' ('Queen of Beauty and Fragrance')

Hybridizer, Date of Introduction: Beluze, 1843
ARS Rating:—
Color: Light pink
Blooms: 1½ to 3½ inches, double, R
Fragrance: Strong
Height: 2 to 3 feet
Hips

Uses: Beds, borders, cutting; climbing form available
Characteristics: Perhaps 'Souvenir de la Malmaison''s former name, 'Queen of Beauty and Fragrance', says it all. Unlike many old roses it takes no more room in a garden than a hybrid Tea. The pale pink flowers bloom in clusters or singly, with a slightly spicy fragrance. The bush has glossy foliage and fairly long stems, which makes the flowers excellent for cutting. Flowers are large, double and often quartered, handsome for exhibition. It is hardy to 10° F.

'Souvenir de la Malmaison' was formerly called 'Queen of Beauty and Fragrance'.

CENTIFOLIA ROSES (CABBAGE ROSES, PROVENCE ROSES)

Cabbage roses have larger outer petals and centers packed with a tight whorl of overlapping petals, much the same as the leaves of a cabbage. Sometimes called Provence roses after the area in southeastern France where they were widely grown, Centifolia roses are thought to have been created around the 16th or 17th century by Dutch hybridizers. The slender bushes have arching canes with large, coarse leaves, wrinkled and serrated. Their large globular, blowsy, many-petaled flowers (often more than 100 petals) were favorite subjects of Dutch artists in the Old Master paintings. They have since become popular in fabric designs and romantic wallpapers, from Victorian times to the present. Most bloom only once, in late spring or early summer. They have large thorns, sometimes hooked. As they age, the flowers develop hollow centers.

A usually sweet, intense and enticing fragrance completes the romantic appeal.

'Tour de Malakoff' ('Black Jack')

Hybridizer, Date of Introduction: Soupert & Notting, 1856
ARS Rating: 7.8
Color: Mauve and mauve blend
Blooms: 3 to 3½ inches, double (45 to 55 petals), O
Fragrance: Strong
Height: 6 to 7 feet
Uses: Beds, borders, pillars
Characteristics: 'Tour de Malakoff' is a Gallica and China hybrid. Two world-renowned experts, the books of both of whom I highly recommend, vehemently disagree as to its beauty. Graham Thomas calls it a "marvel," and Jack Harkness writes, "an arching shrub of wayward disposition and revolting color." Take your pick. Its long, new shoots, with support,

are perfect for a pillar or fence post. The huge flowers bloom once in early summer and, as they age, their prominent veining fades from mauve to grayish mauve. 'Tour de Malakoff' needs very fertile soil and is hardy to −20° F.

'Tour de Malakoff' is a centifolia, a rose with more than a hundred petals.

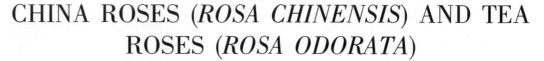

CHINA ROSES (*ROSA CHINENSIS*) AND TEA ROSES (*ROSA ODORATA*)

The Green Rose has small, lime green flowers streaked with reddish brown.

Our modern roses owe their existence to the China roses, the foundation species for modern rose breeding. The China roses are not hardy. They have white, pink, red or purple flowers and may be single, semidouble or double, with from 5 to 50 petals. Most of the flowers have a banana-like fragrance. Some have red-tinged stems and most have large thorns, often curved. They are generally low growing, from 3 to 6 feet, with glossy foliage and, in the fall, large smooth hips.

Arriving in Europe in the early 1800s from their original home in Asia, Tea roses conquered Europe with their fragrance and long bloom. Their flowers are loosely formed of translucent petals in a wide range of colors that includes white, pink, yellow, apricot, fawn, buff and salmon. Their semidouble or double flowers bloom on wide-spreading bushes. They have light green foliage and bright red thorns. Their big drawback is their tenderness; they are extremely susceptible to frost damage and can be grown without protection only in warm climates. It is surmised they were called Tea roses either because they smelled like fresh tea leaves from a newly emptied tea chest or because they traveled on cargo ships of the East India Company, which transported primarily tea to Europe. Their popularity is due to their tendency to repeat bloom. The craze for hybrid roses began with excitement about the potential for long-blooming Tea roses. Since the Tea roses' arrival in Europe, more than 20,000 varieties have been hybridized through breeding programs with Chinese Tea roses.

The Green Rose (*Rosa chinensis viridiflora*)

Hybridizer, Date of Introduction: 1855
ARS Rating: 7.0
Color: Lime green
Blooms: 1 to 1½ inches, double, R
Fragrance: —
Height: 3 feet
Uses: Beds, borders
Characteristics: Known and grown for its strangeness, the Green Rose produces lime green flowers the size of fifty-cent pieces. Against the light green foliage the flowers are camouflaged, reminiscent of battle fatigues, with only a few reddish brown streaks to softly highlight the roses. The rose petals are not petals at all, but multiple sepals. A conversation piece to be sure, and arresting in rose arrangements, but not a beauty in the garden.

'Fantin-Latour'

Hybridizer, Date of Introduction: ca. 1900
ARS Rating: 7.6
Color: Light pink
Blooms: 3 to 3½ inches, double (200+ petals), O
Fragrance: Strong
Height: 5 to 6 feet
Hips
Uses: Beds, borders
Characteristics: 'Fantin-Latour' flowers in midseason. Its light pink blossoms open in a cup shape, and later, when the outer petals reflex, the flower looks more like a hybrid Tea.

'Fantin Latour' blooms with more than 200 fragrant petals.

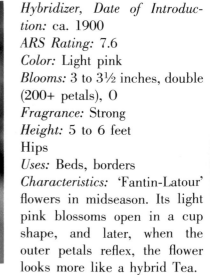

HYBRID PERPETUAL ROSES

From all appearances it seems hybrid perpetuals are crosses between Bourbons and whatever caught the breeder's eye. They were the first repeat bloomers, and a parent of the hybrid Teas. Blooming in spring and fall, with little in between, they have been surpassed in bloom by other modern roses. Their large blooms, up to 7 inches across, are fully double with about a hundred petals in white, pinks and deep maroons. They date from approximately 1840 and were really the first of the modern roses, but are not grown much today. Most have powerful scents and the group encompasses both shrub and climbing roses. As a group they are susceptible to black spot and mildew.

'Ferdinand Pichard'

Hybridizer, Date of Introduction: Tanne, 1921 (France)
ARS Rating: 7.7
Color: Red blend (pink and red striped)
Blooms: 3 inches, double (25 petals), R
Fragrance: Strong
Height: 5 feet
Uses: Cutting, beds, borders
Characteristics: 'Ferdinand Pichard' is of unknown parentage, sometimes classified as a Bourbon, sometimes as a hybrid perpetual. It has tight clusters of raspberry-scented, striped flowers from early summer to fall. They open in midseason with cups of light pink petals streaked with Christmas red and bright pink, as if a paint brush had been carelessly dragged across the surface, leaving some dots, a few dashes of bright pink, and an occasional wide, solid streak of Christmas red. As the rose relaxes and opens further, yellow stamens are revealed. The smooth, large, medium green foliage with serrated edges hides the small, reddish, hooked thorns, so beware. It is an upright shrub with thick, leathery, dark green leaves arranged so the terminal leaflet is drawn out to a fine point.

'Reine des Violettes' ('Queen of Violets')

Hybridizer, Date of Introduction: Millet-Malet, 1860
ARS Rating: 7.1
Color: Mauve and mauve blend
Blooms: 3½ to 4½ inches, quartered (up to 75 petals), R
Fragrance: Strong
Height: 5 to 8 feet
Hips
Uses: Cutting, beds, borders
Characteristics: 'Reine des Violettes' has a richness and depth of color that is arresting whether in the garden or an arrangement. The flowers are carmine, cerise or mauve, later fading to violet shades. Each bloom first opens in a cupped shape and of a dark, yet soft, grape purple hue. The color continues to soften as the cup shape opens out flat. The colors stand out more because of the contrasting darker upper surface and the lighter reverse. They bloom in clusters and each bloom opens flat to a button eye. The leaves are smooth

'Ferdinand Pichard' has raspberry-scented, striped flowers.

with a somewhat grayish cast, the perfect background for the violet flowers. The flowers are sweetly scented on almost thornless canes. It needs excellent soil and continuous dead-heading to produce flowers later in the season because flowering slows as hips are produced. Late flowers are even richer in color than early flowers.

'Reine des Violettes' flowers on almost thornless canes.

NOISETTE ROSES

Noisettes are not often grown today. They have clusters of small flowers. The original Noisette was created by a French immigrant rice grower in Charleston, South Carolina, in the early 19th century, who crossed a *Rosa moschata*, the musk rose, with 'Old Blush', a China rose. The result, 'Blush Noisette', was sent by its creator to his brother in France. The brother, seeing 'Blush Noisette' 's potential, introduced it to commerce. Most Noisettes can't be grown in northern climates without protection. They have smooth, oval leaves from light to medium green, smooth hips and large thorns. The fragrance is one of tea.

Fragrant 'Blush Noisette' blooms nonstop all summer.

'Blush Noisette'

Hybridizer, Date of Introduction: Noisette, 1817
ARS Rating: 6.5
Color: White or near white (light pink)
Blooms: 2 to 2½ inches, double, C
Fragrance: Strong
Height: 3 feet
Disease resistant
Uses: Groundcover, beds, borders
Characteristics: 'Blush Noisette' is sweetly scented of cloves and produces large clusters of flowers (from 8 to 30) throughout the season. The "blush" is in the newly opened double flowers until they age to white. The perfect, pointed, medium pink buds complement the open, light, blush-pink flowers in each cluster. Ultimately the flowers age to white, but I disagree with the American Rose Society's color classification of white for 'Blush Noisette'. I grow 'Blush Noisette' in my garden in an exposed position where cold winds whip in the fall and winter temperatures reach 5° F., and the plant doesn't seem bothered; it is even covered for brief periods with snow. It is not bothered by mildew or black spot, either.

SPECIES ROSES AND THEIR HYBRIDS

Species roses, those found growing in the wild, are single, five-petaled flowers (with *Rosa sericea* an exception, having only 4 petals). They reproduce readily and are true to type when grown from seed, although seedlings, like any children, are not identical to their parents. The colors and scent of species roses are necessary to attract pollinating insects. Conservative botanists estimate there are approximately two dozen distinct botanical species. These are survivors through the centuries, and they don't want to be fed a rich diet, which might kill them. Nearly all are trailing roses capable of crawling along the ground and climbing trees, whichever is necessary to reach the sun and ensure their survival, growing in the wild alongside other shrubs and trees. Species roses native to North America are predominantly pink. Two are of particular note, the Swamp Rose (*Rosa palustris*), which tolerates soggy bogs, and the Prairie Rose (*R. setigera*), growing on arid plains. Species roses from the Middle East are unique in their yellow hues ranging from pale to sulphur; the yellow shades of all species roses today come from the Middle Eastern strains. Asian species, particularly those from China, have contributed to their repeat bloom.

The yellow 'Lady Banks' rose has been a popular choice for southern gardens.

Rosa banksiae lutea 'Lady Banks'

Hybridizer, Date of Introduction: 1824
ARS Rating: 9.0
Color: Medium yellow (light yellow)
Blooms: 1 inch, double (45 to 50 petals), O
Fragrance: Slight
Height: 20 to 30 feet
Hips
Uses: Trellis, house, wall, gazebo
Characteristics: 'Lady Banks' is the double form of a species rose. Flowers bloom on lower side shoots, so don't prune too

closely or they will never bloom. *Rosa banksiae lutea* is a natural mutation of *R. banksiae*. The yellow 'Lady Banks' has been called a "house eater," as it has been known to cover a roof and come down the other side; it can canopy the top of a tree. Both *banksiae* roses, this and *R. banksiae banksiae*, a violet-scented white form, were popular for more than 150 years in southern gardens. Both roses are tender, and neither sets seed.

Rosa eglanteria (Sweetbriar Rose, Eglantine)

Hybridizer, Date of Introduction: Before 1551
ARS Rating: 7.7
Color: Light pink
Blooms: 1 to 2 inches, single (5 to 7 petals), O
Fragrance: Moderate
Height: 9+ feet
Disease resistant
Hips
Uses: Hedges, banks, pillars, groundcover
Characteristics: The Eglantine or Sweetbriar Rose is famous for its apple-scented foliage (fragrance is strongest at the tips of the shoots). Perfumers have tried without success to extract the essence of fragrance from Sweetbriar's leaves. The perfume of the leaves is especially strong after a summer shower. The red, oval hips stay on the bush throughout the winter and until the bush begins to flower again. The single pink flowers are only slightly fragrant, and bloom once for a few weeks. The bush needs to be supported. An arching

shrub, it frequently tosses its branches into a tree and pulls itself up, covering it with thick, thorny growth. When yearly pruned it forms a dense, impenetrable hedge. It is long lived.

Rosa glauca (R. rubrifolia)

Hybridizer, Date of Introduction: Before 1830
ARS Rating: 8.8
Color: Medium pink
Blooms: ½ to 1 inch, single (5 to 7 petals), O
Fragrance: —
Height: 6 to 8 feet
Disease resistant
Hips
Uses: Banks, cutting, beds, borders
Characteristics: R. glauca is unusual for its foliage color. When grown in full sun the new shoots are a deep purple that ages to soft plum washed with silver. In shade the foliage is paler, with a grayish cast. It blooms once early in the season. The clusters of chalky pink flowers contrast nicely with the foliage. The foliage is attractive all season in the garden and in flower arrangements, where it combines beautifully with pink and rosy flowers. The ornamental hips begin a deep maroon and ripen to orange.

Rosa eglanteria is grown more for its fragrant foliage and beautiful hips than its flowers.

Rosa multiflora

Hybridizer, Date of Introduction: 1810
ARS Rating: 6.2
Color: White or near white
Blooms: ½ inch, single (5 petals), O
Fragrance: Moderate
Height: 7 to 12 feet
Disease resistant
Hips
Uses: Groundcover
Characteristics: Brought to this country from Japan, *R.*

Rosa glauca *is unusual for its deep purple foliage washed with silver.*

Rosa multiflora *can be an uninvited guest, naturalizing in woodlands and along highways.*

Rosa wichuraiana *is the father of many of our climbing roses today.*

multiflora was marketed as a "living fence." Unfortunately, it was not realized until later how persistent, vigorous and voracious it is. Having escaped from the gardens where it was first planted, it thrives as an uninvited guest, naturalizing in woodlands, along highways and in many places where it is not wanted. It is difficult to remove as even the smallest root left in the ground can send up shoots and grow into a new bush. It seeds readily, helped by the birds who dine on its hips, and it suckers freely, sending out underground runners and establishing new bushes as it goes, crowding out any weaker plant, shrub or tree in its path. I unsuccessfully struggled for many years to remove all of these shrubs from my woods. Now we have established a peace. I cut them back most years, and pull out seedlings and suckers as I see them. Still, I admire their ability to flower in shade and enjoy their fragrant, single, small, clustered white flowers for a short three weeks in late spring. I dig around them from time to time to keep them in bounds, but my anger is lost in the face of their persistence and beauty.

Rosa wichuraiana (Memorial Rose)

Hybridizer, Date of Introduction: 1891
ARS Rating: 7.8
Color: White or near white
Blooms: 1½ to 2 inches, single (5 petals), O
Fragrance: Moderate
Height: 10 to 20 feet
Disease resistant
Hips
Uses: Groundcover, trellis
Characteristics: Rosa wichuraiana is a creeper that, left to its own devices, can spread its almost thornless canes to 20 feet. It is one of the later-blooming roses, covering itself with clusters of single white flowers. It is the parent of many modern climbing roses. In warm climates it is a semi-evergreen shrub. It produces small, red, oval hips in the fall.

ROSA RUGOSA AND HYBRID RUGOSAS

Rugosas and their hybrids are the quiet ones, the martyrs of the rose world, rarely receiving appreciation or understanding, yet all the while giving freely of their fragrant bloom and making no demands of the gardener. Rugosas are unwelcome in many gardens because of their coarse foliage, shapeless flowers, bristly brown stems and ordinary colors—the country bumpkins, too distant a relative of the Queen of Flowers for welcome. Perhaps their unpleasantly prickly nature is partly to blame; there are prickles all up and down the canes.

Generally rugosas and hybrid rugosas suffer little from black spot and almost never mildew, in spite of frequently dwelling in seaside gardens surrounded by salty air and high humidity. The coarseness of their foliage protects them from fungus spores. If they are infected, they don't appear much bothered, and continue flowering just the same. They are humble, doing jobs that the elegant and parlor roses couldn't and wouldn't do. Because of their easy care and naturally bushy habit, they are favored for highway plantings and provide windblocks on sand dunes. If they become leggy or unshapely they can be cut severely back.

Originally from Asia, the rugosas arrived first in Europe in the last century and were brought with immigrants to American shores; they have naturalized in the Northeast. They offer generous bloom and bright, colorful fall foliage. Not all have ornamental hips. The single-flowered varieties continue blooming as they produce crops of hips the shape and color of cherry tomatoes. The double-flowered varieties also bloom well into autumn but produce fewer hips. Rugosas are an exceptionally winter-hardy family, surviving temperatures from −30° to −40° F.

F. J. Grootendorst

Hybridizer, Date of Introduction: de Goey, 1918
ARS Rating: 8.0
Color: Medium red
Blooms: 1 to 2 inches, double, R, C
Fragrance: —
Height: 5 to 6 feet
Disease resistant
Uses: Pillars, hedges, seaside gardens, borders
Characteristics: Meet the Grootendorsts, a small family of hybrid rugosas within the larger rugosa family. Knowing them will help you understand selected breeding. All have similarly fringed buttons of blossoms that resemble small carnations and bloom in tight clusters, at times with more than 20 flow-

ers per cluster. The differences between Grootendorsts is mainly in their coloration. F. J. Grootendorst was the first, or father, a combination of a Polyantha and a rugosa, with crimson flowers. Both 'Grootendorst Supreme', garnet red, and 'Pink Grootendorst', medium pink, are sports (naturally occurring genetic mutations) of 'F. J. Grootendorst'. 'White Grootendorst' is a sport of 'Pink Grootendorst', and so it goes. 'Grootendorst Supreme' is the smallest of the group, closer to 4 feet, and less vigorous. 'Pink Grootendorst' resembles its parent in every way. The foliage on each bush is lime green. Although the family is without fragrance, they have long, continuous, heavy bloom. They are my old reliables. When every other rose has slowed its bloom, I can always find a cluster of small ruffled flowers on a Grootendorst, perfect for a small bouquet.

Rosa rugosa rubra

Hybridizer, Date of Introduction: 1796
ARS Rating: 8.2
Color: Mauve and mauve blend (deep pink)
Blooms: 2 to 2½ inches, single, R, C
Fragrance: Strong
Height: 4 to 5 feet
Disease resistant
Hips
Uses: Seaside gardens, hedges, borders, groundcover
Characteristics: Rosa rugosa rubra has flamboyant, deep pink, single blossoms washed with purple and decorated with creamy stamens. It suckers readily, even out into a sandy

'F. J. Grootendorst' has fringed buttons of bloom all summer.

beach. Its easy manner makes it a frequent choice by highway planters. It has crinkled foliage and good fall color. The large, round, shiny, orange-scarlet hips clash with the flower's colors to produce an electric mix that brightens a beach. The flesh of the hips is loved by birds, squirrels and cooks. Similar in all respects except color to *Rosa rugosa rubra*, *R. rugosa alba* has poppylike, single white flowers with yellow stamens.

Rosa rugosa rubra will grow easily on a beach, with flowers blooming side by side with the hips.

'Hansa'

Hybridizer, Date of Introduction: Schaum & VanTol, 1905
ARS Rating: 8.5
Color: Medium red (mauve and mauve blend)
Blooms: 3 to 3½ inches, double (35 to 45 petals), R, C
Fragrance: Strong
Height: 5 feet

Disease resistant
Hips
Uses: Seaside gardens, banks, hedges, borders
Characteristics: 'Hansa's' vibrant red-violet flowers are clove scented. She is a vigorous grower, forming dense mounds useful as architectual shapes in a garden or border. Large red hips form in the fall.

'Hansa' is a fragrant, clove-scented rose. Its rough foliage protects it from many pests and diseases.

'Ballerina' blooms with such abundance it resembles a ballerina's tutu.

'Belinda' blooms with large clusters of small, fragrant flowers.

Hybrid Musk Roses

'Ballerina'

Hybridizer, Date of Introduction: J. A. Bentall, 1937
ARS Rating: —
Color: Medium pink
Blooms: 2 inches, single (5 petals), R
Fragrance: Slight
Height: 3 to 4 feet
Disease resistant
Uses: Containers, beds, borders, hedges
Characteristics: 'Ballerina' has dense canes that arch up and cascade down, hidden all the while by flower clusters. Each single, medium pink flower with a white eye may be small, but the clusters are showy from a distance. Pick the end of a stem and you will have an instant bouquet. Although late to open, 'Ballerina' is generous with her blooms, which drape in abundance and resemble a ballerina's skirt—hence her name. Her fragrance is slightly musky and has been compared to that of sweet peas. 'Ballerina' has few thorns and light green, semiglossy foliage.

'Belinda'

Hybridizer, Date of Introduction: Bentall, 1936
ARS Rating: 8.5
Color: Medium pink
Blooms: Under 2 inches, semidouble (12 to 15 petals), R
Fragrance: Slight
Height: 4 to 6 feet
Uses: Beds, borders, hedges, groundcover
Characteristics: When 'Belinda' is in bloom her skirts are completely covered with large clusters of small, fragrant flowers, and it's hard to keep your eyes off her. As wide as she is tall, 'Belinda' can spread to 6 feet with good care.

'Cornelia'

Hybridizer, Date of Introduction: Pemberton, 1925
ARS Rating:—
Color: Pink blend
Blooms: 1 to 2 inches, double (80 to 90 petals), R
Fragrance: Moderate
Height: 5 to 7 feet, higher if trained up a wall

Uses: Beds, borders, climbing, cutting, container

Characteristics: 'Cornelia' is a lovely lady with medium pink flowers accented with flat buttons in their centers. Each cane arches gracefully, covered abundantly with small double blooms; cut a foot and a half off the end of a cane for an instant bouquet. Buds look miniature, only ½ inch high, and equally as wide at the bottom. The perfume has been described by nurseries as "soft, rich and musky." The tiny, hairlike thorns slide easily into unprotected fingers. This is one rose you wear gloves while cutting and arranging. The foliage is a matte, light yellow-green, each small oval leaf looking as though it were cut delicately with pinking shears. Early in the season, 'Cornelia' is a heavy bloomer, the canes brushing the ground from the weight of the many flowers. Later, at summer's end, the flowers bloom in a richer coppery-coral color.

Rosa moyesii 'Geranium'

Hybridizer, Date of Introduction: E. H. Wilson, 1894
ARS Rating:—
Color: Medium red
Blooms: 1¾ to 2½ inches, single (5 petals), O
Fragrance: —
Height: 10 feet
Disease resistant
Hips
Uses: Borders
Characteristics: This is a hybrid _moyesii._ The rich, fire-red flowers blaze for a few short weeks in early summer, but the bush is relighted at summer's

'Cornelia' is a heavy bloomer with a musky perfume.

end by large, red flagon-shaped hips. Each flower bears short, yellow stamens arranged in a perfect circle, like a crown in the center. 'Geranium' is a thornless bush growing on upright, reddish brown canes and clothed in ferny foliage that attractively fills any flower arrangement.

MODERN ROSES

These roses need a regular regime of pampering. Modern roses, of rather complex hybrid origin, bloom over a period of several months. The appeal of the modern roses is their longer petals, high pointed centers, long pointed buds, larger flowers, long straight stems and brilliant and sometimes flamboyant colors and color blends. The insatiable desire for novelty has breeders hybridizing for even more unusual colors— shades of blue, black and butterscotch. Modern roses are admired as buds or in their half-open stage, rather than in full bloom as the old garden roses are.

Many modern roses have been grafted onto the roots of another rose. There are two reasons for this. It is quicker and easier for the commercial grower to produce roses and bring them to market as grafts. Also, some of the hybrids on their own develop spindly root systems and the bushes consequently lack vigor. Breeders solved this problem by grafting flower-bearing branches to the more vigorous roots of such wild roses as _Rosa multiflora._ Roses that have been grafted are easily identified by the knucklelike lump, called a bud union, at the base of the plant. Modern roses grow without protection where winters are mild. In Maine and other northern climates, they can be grown as annuals or with added protection (see page 38).

'Geranium' has fire-red _flowers on thornless canes._

'Cécile Brunner' flowers are small enough to be the perfect boutonniere flower.

'The Fairy' is a good choice for a rose hedge.

Polyantha Roses

Polyantha is Greek for "many blooms." Polyantha roses bloom with large clusters of small flowers (under 2 inches). They are dense and low growing, and can be massed effectively as groundcovers or a low hedge. The colors range from white to deep pink, with a few yellows, salmon and orange. Blooms are single, semidouble or double. As a group they have little or no fragrance. They are one parent of the Floribundas, and most Polyanthas are winter hardy to –20° F.

'Cécile Brunner' ('Mignon', 'The Sweetheart Rose', 'Mlle Cecile Brunner')

Hybridizer, Date of Introduction: Ducher, 1891
ARS Rating: 8.0
Color: Light pink
Blooms: ½ to 1 inch, double, R
Fragrance: Moderate
Height: 2½ to 3 feet
Disease resistant
Uses: Cutting, beds, borders; climbing form available
Characteristics: 'Cécile Brunner' is a Dwarf Polyantha, a distinctive rose easily recognized for its miniature, perfect buds and flowers held well above the foliage on bare branching stems, each with up to a dozen blooms as if to say "pick me." Each bud looks like a miniature hybrid Tea rose, and it is the buds that have earned 'Cécile Brunner' its fame and fortune as the original sweetheart rose worn as a boutonniere. The pale pink buds have yellow streaks at the base; the yellow disappears as the bloom opens to a medium pink center. The bush has a shapely figure with few thorns. A climbing variety is also available, but it isn't as prolific a bloomer. 'Cécile Brunner' is not dependably winter hardy in northern climates.

'The Fairy'

Hybridizer, Date of Introduction: Bentall, 1932
ARS Rating: 8.7
Color: Light pink
Blooms: 1 to 1½ inches, double (24 to 30 petals), R
Fragrance: —
Height: 1½ to 3 feet
Disease resistant
Uses: Bank, hedge, beds, borders
Characteristics: 'The Fairy' is an easy-going, stocky, squat shrub that, when left alone, prefers to be wider than it is tall. It can be highly recommended for its adaptability to poor locations. Later than most roses, it blooms nonstop until well after frost. The miniature flowers bloom in tight clusters, opening a medium pink and quickly fading to light pink, with a good mix of both colors on the bush at all times. The leaves are shiny, small and dark green with good disease resistance.

'Margo Koster'

Hybridizer, Date of Introduction: Koster, 1931
ARS Rating: 7.6
Color: Orange blend (coral/salmon)
Blooms: 1 to 2 inches, semidouble (7 to 12 petals), R
Fragrance: Slight

Height: 1 to 2 feet (shrub)
Uses: Beds, borders, edging; climbing form available
Characteristics: The small, salmon, globe-shaped flowers 'Margo Koster' wears are arresting, delicate, and unique. There is a climbing variety available, which I prefer because the flowers are easier to see and there are many more of them. My climbing 'Margo Koster' was so short at one and two years I pruned off only dead canes. Now, after several years, she is up and over the 6-foot-high garden wall, blooming everywhere on both old and new canes.

'Margo Koster' is unusual with her salmon-colored, globe-shaped roses the size of fifty-cent pieces.

Hybrid Tea Roses

Hybrid Teas, the most popular of all roses, have the widest color range, including many different yellows, bicolors, and blends. Their almost continuous bloom on long upright, straight stems makes them good garden shrubs, as well as the most popular of cut flowers. They have been bred for long, pointed buds with high-centered bloom.

Hybrid Tea roses are the most popular class for exhibition roses and have been so since 1918. As the season progresses, deadhead the roses regularly to promote blooms. When deadheading, cut low to a set of five leaflets or to a leaf junction. This encourages stronger canes and keeps the flowers blooming lower.

'Chicago Peace'®
Hybridizer, Date of Introduction: Johnson, 1962
ARS Rating: 8.2
Awards: Portland Gold Medal 1962
Color: Pink blend (yellow-apricot and pink blend)

Blooms: 5 to 5½ inches, double (50 to 60 petals), R
Fragrance: Slight
Height: 4½ to 5½ feet
Uses: Cutting, beds
Characteristics: 'Chicago Peace' is a sport (chance mutation) of the famous 'Peace', and was discovered by a Chicago gardener. It has a lively color mix blending yellow and apricot with various shades of pink on flowers larger than those of 'Peace'. 'Chicago Peace' is considered by many to be a better rose than its parent, with longer stems, darker coloration and more disease resistance, but the parent has all the fame. Give it winter protection where temperatures drop below 10° F.

'Dainty Bess'
Hybridizer, Date of Introduction: Archer, 1925
ARS Rating: 8.8
Awards: Royal National Rose Society Gold Medal 1925
Color: Light pink
Blooms: 3½ to 4 inches, single (5 petals), R
Fragrance: Slight

'Chicago Peace' is a blend of yellow, apricot and pinks.

'Dainty Bess' has soft pink, ruffled petals and wine-colored stamens.

'Double Delight' is both beautiful and fragrant.

'First Prize' has been the top-rated exhibition rose for nine years.

'Fragrant Cloud' has a tea fragrance.

Height: 3 to 4 feet
Disease resistant
Uses: Beds, borders; climbing form available
Characteristics: With abundant bloom and unusual flowers, 'Dainty Bess' is a favorite of mine. Its large, ruffled, soft pink and silvery petals sharply contrast with wine-colored stamens. I like it the best of the single-flowered hybrid Tea roses. The leathery, green foliage is disease resistant and the canes have few thorns.

'Double Delight'®

Hybridizer, Date of Introduction: Swim and Ellis, 1977
ARS Rating: 8.8
Awards: AARS 1977, Baden-Baden Gold Medal 1976, Rome Gold Medal 1976
Color: Red blend
Blooms: 5½ inches, double (35 to 40+ petals), R, C
Fragrance: Strong
Height: 3 to 4 feet
Uses: Cutting, beds; climbing form available
Characteristics: A delight for both its beauty and fragrance, 'Double Delight' is a distinctive and popular rose. It blooms in endless profusion throughout the season. When first open, the blossoms have deep-ruby-edged outer petals with center petals a buttery yellow blending to clear white and tipped with cherry red. The fragrance is strong and spicy. The form of the rose has changed somewhat over the years—no one knows why.

'First Prize'

Hybridizer, Date of Introduction: Boerner, 1970
ARS Rating: 8.9
Awards: AARS 1970, ARS Gertrude M. Hubbard Gold Medal 1971
Color: Pink blend
Blooms: 5 to 6 inches, double (25 to 35 petals), R
Fragrance: Slight
Height: 2½ to 3 feet tall
Uses: Cutting, beds; climbing form available
Characteristics: 'First Prize' is the highest-rated hybrid Tea, and the top-rated exhibition rose for nine years in a row. It is a prolific bloomer with up to 50 flowers a season. The flowers are deep rose pink on the inside, silvery pink outside. The long stems make it good for cutting and if cut in tight bud, the flowers have a long life. It is prone to both black spot and mildew. Winter protection is needed below 30° F.

'Fragrant Cloud' ('Duftwolke', 'Nuage Perfume')

Hybridizer, Date of Introduction: Tantau 1967
ARS Rating: 8.0
Awards: Royal National Rose Society's President's International Trophy 1964, Portland Gold Medal 1966, 1986 Rose of the Year, James Alexander Gamble Rose Fragrance Medal 1969
Color: Orange-red
Blooms: 4 to 5 inches, double (25 to 30 petals), R
Fragrance: Strong
Height: 4 to 5 feet
Uses: Cutting, beds
Characteristics: A profuse bloomer with a strong tea fragrance, 'Fragrant Cloud''s coral red color screeches amid its dark foliage. The color fades

a few days after opening, and the leaves cover and hide the canes; as a rosarian would say, "the bush is well clothed." The perfume of one flower will fill a room with its intense old-rose scent. The foliage is susceptible to black spot. Winter protection is needed below 10° F.

'Garden Party'

Hybridizer, Date of Introduction: Swim, 1959
ARS Rating: 8.4
Awards: Bagatelle Gold Medal 1959, AARS 1960
Color: White or near white (pink blend)
Blooms: 4 to 5 inches, double (25 to 30 petals), R, C
Fragrance: Slight
Height: 4 to 6 feet
Uses: Cutting, beds
Characteristics: 'Garden Party' is a popular exhibition rose with flowers that open pale yellow and fade to white with tinges of pink. In fall the colors are deeper. The foliage is dark green on top, reddish underneath.

'Granada' ('Donatella')

Hybridizer, Date of Introduction: Lindquist, 1963
ARS Rating: 8.4
Awards: AARS 1964, Gamble Fragrance Medal 1968
Color: Red blend (pink blend)
Blooms: 3 to 4 inches, double (18 to 25 petals), R
Fragrance: Strong
Height: 4 to 6 feet
Uses: Bedding, cutting; climbing form available
Characteristics: 'Granada' features an intense color blend with a peachy yellow in the center and a loud orange-peach

on the outer petals, with a little gold, red and pink mixed between. It has a strong, spicy fragrance, and blooms prolifically on single stems or in clusters on very thorny canes. It is prone to mildew and needs winter protection below 20° F.

'Marijke Koopman'

Hybridizer, Date of Introduction: Fryer, 1979
ARS Rating: 7.8
Awards: The Hague Gold Medal 1978
Color: Medium pink
Blooms: 4 to 5 inches, clusters of double flowers (25 petals), R
Fragrance: Strong
Height: 4 to 5 feet
Disease resistant
Uses: Cutting, beds, borders
Characteristics: Everywhere I've bumped into 'Marijke Koopman' she was turning heads as a prolific bloomer on a full-bodied, upright bush. Her large, sharp, rosy pink flowers could stop you in your tracks. This is one of the brightest pinks. 'Marijke Koopman' is a good rose for the show table with long, pointed buds, three to five flowers in each cluster, dark leathery foliage veined with red and red prickles on the stems.

'Medallion'®

Hybridizer, Date of Introduction: Warriner, 1973
ARS Rating: 7.1
Awards: AARS 1973, Portland Gold Medal 1972
Color: Apricot and apricot blend
Blooms: Up to 6 to 7 inches, double (20 to 25 petals), R
Fragrance: Strong
Height: 3 to 5 feet
Uses: Cutting, beds

'Garden Party' is a pale yellow with tinges of pink.

'Granada' boasts an intense color blend.

'Marijke Koopman' is a prolific bloomer.

'Medallion' produces large flowers up to 7 inches across.

'Mister Lincoln' is the most popular red rose.

Characteristics: 'Medallion' has among the largest flowers, in delicate shades of apricot-pink with petals loosely arranged. The buds are exceptionally long, and the first row of petals must be unfurling before the rose is cut or they won't open at all. The fragrance is strong and fruity. 'Medallion' prefers climates with mild, cool weather and is not reliably hardy without protection.

'Mister Lincoln'®

Hybridizer, Date of Introduction: Swim & Weeks, 1964
ARS Rating: 8.9
Awards: AARS 1965
Color: Dark red
Blooms: 5 to 6 inches, double (30 to 40 petals), R
Fragrance: Strong
Height: 4½ to 5½ feet
Uses: Cutting, beds; climbing form available
Characteristics: 'Mister Lincoln' is a moderate bloomer, but a single flower perfumes an entire room. It boasts one of the most popular reds, and each elegantly pointed bud is per-

fection. The dark red flowers fade to an unpleasant purple-blue. 'Mister Lincoln' grows as a vigorous bush with reddish stems and dark green foliage. It is hardy to 10° F. without protection.

'Olympiad'™® ('Olympiade'®)

Hybridizer, Date of Introduction: McGredy, 1982
ARS Rating: 8.3
Awards: AARS 1984, Portland Gold Medal 1985
Color: Medium red
Blooms: 4 to 5 inches, double (24 to 30 petals), R
Fragrance: Slight
Height: 4 to 5 feet
Uses: Cutting, beds
Characteristics: The urn-shaped buds are dark red, almost black, and when open the flowers are of a classic spiral form and the color and texture of red velvet, all surrounded by gray-green foliage. It seems a sin to grow a red rose without a strong fragrance, but 'Olympiad' 's beauty and agreeable nature help to overlook this flaw. The flowers hold their color well, and when they start to wither, drop to the ground rather than hanging in an unsightly fashion on the bush.

'Paradise'™® ('Burning Sky')

Hybridizer, Date of Introduction: Weeks, 1978
ARS Rating: 8.6
Awards: AARS 1979, Portland Gold Medal 1979
Color: Mauve and mauve blend
Blooms: 3½ to 4½ inches, double (25 to 30 petals), R, C
Fragrance: Strong
Height: 4 to 4½ feet

'Olympiad' is the color and texture of red velvet.

Uses: Cutting, beds; climbing form available

Characteristics: 'Paradise' can't be ignored with its bold color scheme. You either love it or hate it. It is considered by many to be the best mauve rose, with lavender-pink inner petals, red edges and strong pink outer petals. It is hardy to 20° F.

'Peace' ('Gioia', 'Gloria Dei', 'Mme. A. Meilland')

Hybridizer, Date of Introduction: Meilland, 1945
ARS Rating: 8.7
Awards: AARS 1946, Portland Gold Medal 1944, American Rose Society Gold Medal 1947, The Golden Rose of The Hague 1965
Color: Yellow blend
Blooms: 5 to 6 inches, double (40 to 45 petals), R
Fragrance: Slight
Height: 4 to 6 feet
Uses: Cutting, beds; climbing form available
Characteristics: Named to commemorate the end of World War II, 'Peace' is a stunning, multicolored blend with golden yellow at the base and rose-pink edges. The areas of rosy pink become larger as the petals unfold. This is the most popular rose of the century. Winter protection is needed below 15° F.

'Precious Platinum' ('Opa Potschke', 'Red Star')

Hybridizer, Date of Introduction: Dickson, 1974
ARS Rating: 7.9
Awards:—
Color: Medium red

Blooms: 3½ inches, double (35 to 40 petals), R, C
Fragrance: Slight
Height: 4 feet
Disease resistant
Uses: Cutting, beds
Characteristics: 'Precious Platinum' is a confusing name for a red rose, but it was named for a company rather than the color of its blooms, which are a clear medium red. It is a good all-around garden rose with a bushy habit. Although not noted for its show qualities, it makes a good cut flower and is one of the fastest reblooming hybrid Teas. Hardy to 10° F. without protection.

'Pristine'®

Hybridizer, Date of Introduction: Warriner, 1978
ARS Rating: 8.7
Color: White or near white
Blooms: 4½ to 6 inches, double (30 to 35 petals), R

'Paradise' has one of the boldest color blends.

'Peace' is the most popular rose of this century.

'Precious Platinum' is one of the fastest reblooming roses.

'Pristine' opens from an ivory bud to a blushing pink blossom.

'Sheer Bliss' blooms on long stems excellent for cutting.

'Tiffany' has been a popular rose for a quarter of a century.

'Touch of Class' flowers change color as they age, ending up a soft salmon.

Fragrance: Slight
Height: 3 to 4½ feet
Uses: Cutting, beds
Characteristics: A top-rated exhibition rose, blooming one flower to a stem, with long, tapered, ivory buds that open into white spirals, blushing a soft pink at the outer edges of the petals. Large, deep green, glossy leaves on almost thornless canes.

'Sheer Bliss'

Hybridizer, Date of Introduction: Warriner, 1985
ARS Rating: 7.6
Awards: AARS 1987, Japan Gold Medal 1984
Color: White (pink blend)
Blooms: 4 to 5 inches, double (35 petals), R
Fragrance: Strong
Height: 4 to 4½ feet
Uses: Cutting, beds
Characteristics: 'Sheer Bliss' is just that, with delicately beautiful, creamy white flowers blushed with soft pink at the center. The blooms are on long stems, good for cutting, and the bush has a tidy, upright habit.

'Tiffany'

Hybridizer, Date of Introduction: Lindquist, 1954
ARS Rating: 8.4
Awards: AARS 1955, Portland Gold Medal 1954
Color: Pink blend
Blooms: 4 to 5 inches, double (25 to 30 petals), R, C
Fragrance: Strong
Height: 2½ to 4 feet
Uses: Cutting, beds; climbing form available
Characteristics: 'Tiffany' is a blend of medium to deep pink with yellow at the base. It has been popular for more than a quarter of a century with its fragrant, profuse blooms, light green foliage and show-quality flowers.

'Touch of Class'™® ('Marechale Le Clerc')

Hybridizer, Date of Introduction: Kriloff, 1984
ARS Rating: 8.3
Awards: AARS 1986, Portland Gold Metal 1988
Color: Orange-pink
Blooms: 4½ to 5½ inches, double (30 to 35 petals), R
Fragrance: Slight
Height: 4 feet
Uses: Cutting, beds
Characteristics: The buds are salmon-pink, opening to a soft pink inside with a fluorescent coral on the outer petals. The sun quickly takes the color as the flower ages until the bloom is left a soft salmon. As a cut flower in the bud stage it will keep for a week or longer but will not continue to open. The stems are strong and straight with large thorns. The foliage is "staircased," with larger leaves at the base and progressively smaller ones toward the top. New stems and foliage are reddish throughout the season, contrasting nicely with the older green foliage. This has been a top-rated exhibition rose as it consistently produces flowers with good form and high, beautifully spiraled centers.

'Tropicana' ('Super Star')

Hybridizer, Date of Introduction: Tantau, 1960
ARS Rating: 8.3
Awards: Royal National Rose

Society President's International Trophy 1960, AARS 1963, American Rose Society Gold Medal 1967, Portland Gold Medal 1961
Color: Orange-red (orange blend)
Blooms: 5 inches, double (30 to 35 petals), R, C
Fragrance: Strong
Height: 4 to 5 feet

Uses: Cutting, beds
Characteristics: 'Tropicana' was the first of the orange-red hybrid Teas. The flowers have a strong fruity fragrance and are long-lasting, holding their intense coral color well as they bloom on vigorous, thorny bushes.

'Tropicana' is the first of the orange-red hybrid Tea roses.

FLORIBUNDA ROSES

For masses of summer-long color, floribundas take the prize. Named "flowers in abundance" in Latin, during rose season, floribundas bloom everywhere almost continuously, taking only a short midwinter break in southern climates, and so endearing themselves to gardeners everywhere. Floribundas are the most adaptable of the modern roses, needing only ordinary care. They are compatible and thrive in combination with other plants. Their pedigree brings together the best traits of hardy Polyanthas and many of the long-blooming ancestors of the hybrid Tea. The Polyanthas (bred from the sturdy stock of *Rosa chinensis*, *R. moschata* and *R. multiflora*) donate their clusters of small blossoms to combine with the hybrid Tea's larger flowers and longer stems to produce clusters of flowers 2 to 4 inches across on moderately long stems. The buds of the floribunda are long and pointed, the bushes compact—2 to 3 feet tall and equally wide. The blossoms may be single, semi-double or heavily double.

'Angel Face'

Hybridizer, Date of Introduction: Swim & Weeks, 1968
ARS Rating: 8.2
Awards: AARS 1969, John Cook medal for fragrance 1971
Color: Mauve and mauve blend
Blooms: 3 to 4 inches, double (35 to 40 petals), R, C
Fragrance: Strong
Height: 2 to 3 feet
Uses: Cutting, beds; climbing form available
Characteristics: 'Angel Face''s fame and fortune are in her unusual, deep-toned, lavender-waved petals edged in ruby red and her full-bodied, spicy fragrance. While the rose is classified as mauve, the bluish-purple undertones are strong. There is nothing washed out or weepy about this rose.

'Betty Prior'

Hybridizer, Date of Introduction: Prior, 1935
ARS Rating: 8.0

Awards: Royal National Rose Society Gold Medal 1933
Color: Medium pink
Blooms: 2 to 3 inches, single, R, C
Fragrance: Slight
Height: 4 to 5+ feet
Disease resistant
Uses: Hedges, beds, borders
Characteristics: As close to foolproof as it gets when it comes to growing roses, 'Betty Prior' with her phenomenal flower production is on almost every expert's list of top ten disease-resistant roses. This is the last rose in my garden to stop flowering. Her clusters can range from 11 to 21 flowers of open, single pink blossoms. The petals are held up and are saucer-shaped, medium pink on the inside and darker pink on the outside. Individual petals are heart-shaped, and they are decorative scattered on a tabletop. Among the tallest of the floribundas, 'Betty Prior' is a beautiful sight in winter when cold weather changes her green stems to burgundy-red to contrast with the snow. 'Betty

'Angel Face' has a full-bodied, spicy fragrance.

'Betty Prior' is one of the easiest, longest blooming and most disease-resistant roses.

'Eyepaint'® ('Eye Paint', 'Tapis Persan')

Hybridizer, Date of Introduction: McGredy, 1975
ARS Rating: 8.0
Awards: Baden-Baden Gold Medal 1978, Belfast Gold Medal 1978
Color: Red blend
Blooms: 2½ inches, single (5 to 7 petals), R
Fragrance: —
Height: 3 to 4 feet
Uses: Hedges, landscaping
Characteristics: The scarlet eyes with whitish yellow centers and ruffled petals make 'Eyepaint' a showy garden shrub. It has such bushy growth that it is sometimes classified as a shrub. It is susceptible to black spot.

'Eyepaint' is a showy shrub for the garden.

'Gene Boerner' blooms in clusters of flowers.

'Gene Boerner'

Hybridizer, Date of Introduction: Boerner, 1968
ARS Rating: 8.6
Awards: AARS 1969
Color: Medium pink
Blooms: 2½ to 3½ inches, double (35 petals), R
Fragrance: Slight
Height: 4 to 5 feet
Uses: Cutting, beds
Characteristics: 'Gene Boerner' has high-centered, vibrant pink flowers that are slightly luminous. They have the form of hybrid Tea flowers but usually bloom in clusters. The bush grows taller than most floribundas and remains slender. It has few thorns. 'Gene Boerner' is named for the American hybridizer who has done more than anyone in the development of floribundas in the United States. It needs winter protection where temperatures drop below 20° F.

Prior' forms bushy, full shrubs and looks as great planted *en masse* as in an island bed in the middle of New York City's Columbus Circle, where she happily lives with total disregard for pollution, high winds and little care. This rose is winter hardy without protection to 15° F.

'Iceberg' ('Schnee-wittchen', 'Fee des Neiges')

Hybridizer, Date of Introduction: Kordes, 1958
ARS Rating: 8.7
Awards: Royal National Rose Society Gold Medal 1958
Color: White or near white
Blooms: 2½ to 4 inches, double (30 petals), R
Fragrance: Slight
Height: 4 feet
Disease resistant
Uses: Hedges, beds, borders
Characteristics: 'Iceberg' is the most popular white floribunda. The buds are the palest pink, opening to white, double blossoms with golden stamens. The contrast of the pink buds to the white flowers on the same bush is very pretty indeed. Each flower opens flat with a hint of pink in the center. If lightly pruned, this rose can be grown as a shrub.

'Sexy Rexy'® ('Heckenzauber')

Hybridizer, Date of Introduction: McGredy, 1984
ARS Rating: 8.1
Awards: New Zealand 1984
Color: Medium pink
Blooms: 3 inches wide, double, R
Fragrance: Slight
Height: 2 to 3 feet
Uses: Hedges, beds, containers
Characteristics: 'Sexy Rexy', in keeping with his name, is a prolific producer of blooms. Up to 100 flowers can be found on one spray in early summer. The flowers have ruffled, medium pink petals. The bush has a spreading habit.

'Simplicity'

Hybridizer, Date of Introduction: Warriner, 1978
ARS Rating: 8.0
Awards: New Zealand Gold Medal 1976
Color: Medium pink
Blooms: 3 to 4 inches, semi-double (18 to 20 petals), R, C
Fragrance: Slight
Height: 3 to 5 feet
Disease resistant
Uses: Hedges, beds, borders, cutting
Characteristics: 'Simplicity' is a landscaping rose with classic pink flowers. Four 'Simplicity' shrubs have surrounded a sundial in the center of my herb

'Iceberg' is pink in bud and white in flower.

'Sexy Rexy' blooms with as many as 100 flowers on one spray.

'Simplicity' combines easily with other plants.

'Sunsprite', a bright yellow, is unusual in that it doesn't fade.

garden for 10 years. They have never known chemical sprays nor commercial fertilizers, and yet they have been dependably floriferous. One summer, after a particurlarly severe winter, the shrubs looked as though they needed replacing. Not having the time to pull them out, I planted the annual love-in-a-puff so its vines could cover the distressed canes of the roses. The following spring I intended to replace them, but they had recovered and were back to their healthy, beautiful bloom. 'Simplicity' needs protection where winter temperatures fall below 15° F.

'Sunsprite' ('Friesia')

Hybridizer, Date of Introduction: Kordes, 1977
ARS Rating: 8.8
Awards: Baden-Baden Gold Medal 1972
Color: Deep yellow
Blooms: 3 to 4 inches, R
Fragrance: Strong
Height: 3 to 5 feet
Disease resistant
Uses: Beds, cutting; climbing form available
Characteristics: 'Sunsprite' has prolific bloom in the knock-'em dead shade of brightest yellow that doesn't fade. On a sunny day, even from a distance, a clump of bushes can be blinding. It does, however, drop its petals in a hurry, and the flowers are not long lasting on the bush or in the vase.

GRANDIFLORA ROSES

'Pink Parfait' blooms both singly and in clusters.

For elegant flowers, the grandifloras are ranked among the best. Within the group, blooms range from 3 to 5 inches across and may be one to a stem or clustered, opening from candelabra-like buds. The appearance of their foliage, thorns, buds and blossoms is very similar to that of the hybrid Teas from which they were bred. Grandifloras vary in height, averaging from 3 to 6 feet, but are often taller. Their colors are simple—there are no lavenders to date, and very few mixed colors. They are ideal for the back of a border, as an accent or to block a view. The flowers are good for cutting.

'Gold Medal'®

Hybridizer, Date of Introduction: Christensen, 1982
ARS Rating: 8.0
Awards: New Zealand Gold Medal 1963
Color: Deep yellow (yellow blend)
Blooms: 3½ inches, double (35 to 40 petal)
Fragrance: Slight
Height: 4½ to 5½ feet
Uses: Beds, cutting
Characteristics: 'Gold Medal' is of an intense yellow-gold. The flowers exhibit good hybrid Tea form and bloom singly and in clusters. As the flower ages it changes from a deep yellow-gold to a paler yellow, the petals all tipped with pink. Many shades of yellow are present on the bush at the same time. The buds are a deep gold with red edges that soften as they open to soft pink. This rose was originally passed over by the AARS but later received many awards. It is, however, susceptible to powdery mildew and black spot. It is one of the hardier grandifloras.

'Pink Parfait'

Hybridizer, Date of Introduction: Swim, 1960
ARS Rating: 8.6
Awards: AARS 1961, Portland Gold Medal 1959, Baden-Baden Gold Medal 1959, Royal National Rose Society Gold Medal 1962
Color: Pink blend
Blooms: 3 to 4 inches, double (20 to 25 petals), C, R
Fragrance: Slight

Height: 2½ to 4½ feet
Uses: Beds, cutting
Characteristics: 'Pink Parfait' is a blend of light and medium shades of pink. The blooms have the high centers loved by exhibitors. It blooms sometimes singly, sometimes in clusters.

'Queen Elizabeth'® ('The Queen Elizabeth Rose')

Hybridizer, Date of Introduction: Lammerts, 1954
ARS Rating: 9.2
Awards: Portland Gold Medal 1954, AARS 1955, Royal National Rose Society President's International Trophy 1955, American Rose Society Gold Medal 1957, Golden Rose of the Hague 1968
Color: Medium pink
Blooms: 3 to 4 inches, double, R, C
Fragrance: Moderate
Height: 6+ feet
Disease resistant
Uses: Beds, borders, cutting; climbing form available
Characteristics: 'Queen Elizabeth', the first official member of this class, remains the best-loved and most widely grown of the grandifloras. The medium pink flowers are high-centered and cupped, blooming singly or in small clusters. This rose has long, often thornless, stems that reach higher than 6 feet.

'Gold Medal' has flowers with many different shades of yellow blooming at the same time.

MINIATURE ROSES

You have to admire the exquisite detail of a rose in miniature. These roses may look fragile, but they are tough, hardy plants and extremely versatile for having been bred from various large, vigorous and hardy species roses such as *Rosa multiflora*, *R. roxburghii*, *R. rugosa* and *R. wichuraiana*. Many miniature roses are less than a foot high. Miniature roses were known as fairy roses in the 18th and 19th centuries. Half a century ago, though they were growing in popularity, miniatures were all very similar, 8 to 10 inches high, available in limited colors and with flowers the size of quarters. Today, there is never a dull moment for one who collects minis. They mimic their larger cousins the climbers, the moss roses, the old-fashioned roses and the hybrid Teas, among others, and display the same wide range of colors and flower shapes as the other varieties, many with fragrance. The habits have changed, too. Some have a 3- to 4-foot spread and are covered with flowers 2 inches across. Others are only 6 inches high with ½-inch flowers. The most diminutive are referred to as micro-minis.

You must not, however, be fooled by their names. Some, such as the climber 'Red Cascade', can grow 20 feet tall and bloom all season, covered with miniature flowers. The size of many miniatures when grown in especially nutritious soil can be larger. Climate, the amount of water available and maintenance influence a rose's behavior. They are ideal for windowboxes, rock gardens, massing as a groundcover and growing on indoor windowsills or under lights. Buy

'Queen Elizabeth' is the most widely grown of the grandifloras.

'Magic Carrousel' is covered with tiny buttons of flowers when in full bloom.

The red miniature rose 'Over the Rainbow' and the yellow 'Rise 'n' Shine' share a container.

some in the fall to grow indoors, and the following spring set them out in the garden. Miniatures have never been found in the wild and their origin remains unknown. Evidence points toward China, where miniatures were featured in ancient drawings.

'Magic Carrousel'®

Hybridizer, Date of Introduction: Moore, 1972
ARS Rating: 9.1
Awards: ARS Award of Excellence Winner 1975
Color: Red blend
Blooms: 1¾ to 2 inches, semi-double (12 to 20 petals), R, C
Fragrance: Slight
Height: 25 to 30 inches
Disease resistant
Uses: Beds, borders, cutting, containers, houseplants
Characteristics: Looking like a hybrid Tea, 'Magic Carrousel' is a bicolor, unique and popu-

lar for the rosy red edges that brighten the white flowers. Sometimes the flowers bloom singly, one flower per stem; at other times they bloom in clusters of three. The fragrance, though slight, is reminiscent of violets. Frequently a prize winner in competition.

'Over the Rainbow'

Hybridizer, Date of Introduction: Moore, 1972
ARS Rating: 8.3
Awards: ARS Award of Excellence 1975
Color: Red blend
Blooms: 1¼ to 1½ inches, double (28 to 35 petals), R
Fragrance: Slight
Height: 12 to 14 inches
Uses: Beds, hanging baskets, containers, edging, houseplants; climbing form available
Characteristics: As colorful as its name implies, 'Over the Rainbow' has red and pink centers in bright contrast to the yellow undersides of the petals. The yellow matures to white in a few days and is a good contrast with the dark green foliage. The climbing form can grow to 5 feet.

'Red Cascade'

Hybridizer, Date of Introduction: Moore, 1976
ARS Rating: 7.5
Awards: An Award of Excellence Winner 1976
Color: Dark red
Blooms: 1½ inches, double (35 petals), R
Fragrance: Slight
Height: 6 to 20 feet
Uses: Hanging baskets, hedges, banks, groundcover, pillars
Characteristics: 'Red Cascade' is a climbing miniature. On my

visits to southern rose gardens, I found this rose stood out everywhere it was grown, one time holding a bank, another time as a hedge, and as a single bush surrounding and reaching over a 10-foot-tall lamp post. It forms a thicket of deep green foliage with bright red, button flowers. I'm told it grows to 20 feet in the South. It sprouts many lateral (side) shoots along each cane, which help support it and give it a full figure. It is susceptible to mildew.

'Rise 'n' Shine' ('Golden Sunblaze')

Hybridizer, Date of Introduction: Moore, 1977

ARS Rating: 9.1

Awards: An Award of Excellence Winner 1978

Color: Medium yellow (deep yellow)

Blooms: 1½ to 2 inches, double (35 petals), R, C

Fragrance: Slight

Height: 12 to 15 inches

Disease resistant

Uses: Beds, borders, containers, edging; climbing form available

Characteristics: 'Rise 'n' Shine' has perfect show form with perfect flowers. The large foliage is an ideal background for the small size of the buds.

A photograph of 'Rise 'n' Shine' appears on page 74.

'Red Cascade' is a versatile miniature climber.

SHRUB ROSES

Shrub roses are grouped for the tough, hardy, "fend for themselves" attitude they share rather than for similarity of appearance. This is a catch all group of roses that give much beauty while causing little trouble, and they are used in many of the same ways as other flowering shrubs. Many grow well even in poor soil and are hardy to –30° F. (occasionally –40° F.). They can be used for screen planting, hedges, and massing of bold or soft colors, as there is great variation within the group. They range in height from 2 to 10 feet, some with coarse foliage and some with smooth. The flowers vary, with single, semidouble and double flowers, the newer introductions resembling the hybrid Tea in form. Many, but not all, have hips, and the fragrance varies from none to strong.

'Belle Story'®

Hybridizer, Date of Introduction: Austin, 1985

ARS Rating:—

Color: Light pink

Blooms: 3½ to 4½ inches, double (100+ petals), R

Fragrance: Strong

Height: 5 feet

Disease resistant

Uses: Beds, cutting, landscaping

Characteristics: 'Belle Story'® is a charmer whose peachy pink color captures the heart of all who see her. Each flower's rounded, full figure is bejeweled upon opening with a tangle of golden stamens. The shrub forms a mound as high as it is wide with few thorns and medium green foliage.

'Blanc Double de Coubert'

Hybridizer, Date of IntroducARS Rating: 7.8

Color: White or near white

Blooms: 2 to 3 inches, semidouble (18 to 24 petals), R

Fragrance: Strong

'Belle Story' opens to reveal a tangle of golden stamens.

'Blanc Double de Coubert' is one of the earliest roses to bloom.

'Bonica' is known for her beauty, disease resistance, and easy-going ways.

the earliest roses to bloom, and the first flowers are fading before neighboring rose bushes open. The dazzling, snowy white petals are loosely arranged and slightly pleated, looking even a little messy, but they bloom continuously. It is a robust grower, sending out runners. The runners can be dug and given to friends, placed elsewhere in the garden or left to enlarge the existing clump. Each bush is almost as wide as it is tall. The dead flowers cling to the bush like wads of wet tissue paper and call for regular clean up. 'Blanc Double de Coubert' is renowned for its sweet, strong fragrance. Bright orange-scarlet hips, round and large, form in the fall, but they are not as profuse as on species rugosas.

'Bonica'™®, ('Meidomonac', 'Bonica 82'®, 'Demon')

Hybridizer, Date of Introduction: Meilland, 1985
ARS Rating: 8.0

Height: 3 to 7 feet
Disease resistant
Hips
Uses: Banks, hedges, landscaping, mixed border
Characteristics: This is one of

'Golden Wings' is a prolific bloomer.

Awards: AARS 1987, All-Deutsche Rosenneuheiten-prufung 1983
Color: Medium pink
Blooms: 2 to 3 inches, double R, C
Fragrance: Slight
Height: 4 to 5 feet
Disease resistant
Uses: Beds, borders, landscaping, hedges, groundcover, containers
Characteristics: 'Bonica' is a modern trouble-free rose rarely bothered by any diseases. Large clusters of medium pink flowers bloom freely. I grow a clematis on one of these roses and it blooms beautifully with the rose without hurting the bush.

'Golden Wings'

Hybridizer, Date of Introduction: Shepherd, 1956
ARS Rating: 8.5
Awards: American Rose Society Gold Medal 1956
Color: Medium yellow
Blooms: 4 to 5 inches, single (5 to 10 petals), R
Fragrance: Slight
Height: 4 to 8 feet
Hips
Uses: Borders, banks, hedges, landscaping
Characteristics: 'Golden Wings' is the yellow rose rated highest by the ARS. It has large, single, canary yellow blossoms with showy amber stamens. Often it has more than 5 large petals, and the flowers are borne singly or in clusters. A profuse bloomer, 'Golden Wings' is one of the earliest to bloom and among the last to stop. The flowers are followed by orange-red hips.

'Constance Spry'®

Hybridizer, Date of Introduction: Austin, 1961
ARS Rating:—
Color: Light pink
Blooms: 4½ to 5 inches, double (45 to 55 petals), O
Fragrance: Strong
Height: 6 to 7 feet
Disease resistant
Uses: Climbing, shrub, landscape, back of the border
Characteristics: 'Constance Spry'® is the first of the English roses series, a cross between 'Belle Isis', a Gallica, and 'Dainty Maid', a floribunda. She is reminiscent of cabbage roses with her old-fashioned, fully double, bright pink flowers. Her heavy flowers hang on droopy necks, forming a cascade of 6 to 7 feet. It can be grown as a climber to 15 feet tall. Her fragrance is described as myrrh.

'Graham Thomas'®

Hybridizer, Date of Introduction: Austin, 1983
ARS Rating: 8.0
Color: Deep yellow
Blooms: 4 to 5 inches, double, R
Fragrance: Strong
Height: 8 feet
Disease resistant
Uses: Beds, borders, landscaping, cutting, containers
Characteristics: 'Graham Thomas', named after the famous English rosarian, has beautiful, sunny yellow flowers with the old roses' cupped shape, fragrance and vigor. The buds are apricot-pink. The upright slender bush will grow 5 feet wide, so give it room.

'Mary Rose'®

Hybridizer, Date of Introduction: Austin, 1983
ARS Rating:—
Color: Medium pink
Blooms: 4 to 4½ inches, double, R, C
Fragrance: Strong
Height: 4 feet
Disease resistant
Uses: Beds, borders, cutting, landscaping
Characteristics: A classic Austin rose with the fragrance of the old Damasks, 'Mary Rose'® is early to begin blooming and late to stop. The cupped, light pink flowers become globe shaped when fully open. The blooms are clustered 2 to 5 to a stem. Often, a medium pink bud rests alongside a full bloom, which makes a pretty picture when cut for a single rose vase. A small shrub reaching 4 feet by 4 feet, it has dull green foliage that makes it easy to combine with other shrubs or plant in a mixed border or as a specimen shrub.

'Sea Foam'®

Hybridizer, Date of Introduction: Schwartz, 1964
Awards: Rome Gold Medal in 1964, ARS David Fuerstenberg Prize in 1968
ARS Rating: 7.5
Color: White (light pink)
Blooms: 2½ inches, double, R, C
Fragrance: Slight
Height: 8 to 12 feet
Disease resistant
Uses: Beds, borders, hedges, standards, groundcover, bank
Characteristics: Pink in bud, 'Sea Foam'® opens to light pink flowers that whiten as they age. The flowers bloom in clusters and are abundant. This is a carefree shrub I highly recommend.

'Constance Spry' is the first of the modern English roses.

'Graham Thomas' is named after the famous English rosarian.

'Sea Foam' is a carefree shrub rose.

'Mary Rose'™ is a new English rose with the perfume of the old Damask roses.

CLIMBING ROSES, RAMBLER ROSES AND PILLAR ROSES

'Aloha' is a climbing hybrid Tea rose.

Roses grown as climbers are grouped by common characteristics. The large-flowered climbers have flexible canes and usually grow from 6 to 15 feet tall. Their blossoms may be anywhere from 2 to 6 inches across. Some bloom heavily in early spring with few, if any, flowers later. Others have been bred for a heavy spring crop, a few intermittent blooms over the summer and, when the nights again turn cool, another heavy crop of blooms. Climbing hybrid Teas are the result of sports of unusually long-stemmed bushes selected to be grown as climbers. In many cases they have fewer flowers and are not as hardy as the hybrid Teas from which they were derived.

Ramblers are roses with canes that grow 10 to 20 feet a year, usually with dense clusters of small flowers each up to 2 inches across. They need open spaces, with good air circulation to control their susceptibility to mildew. Many varieties spend all their energy their first year in reaching upward, with few or no blooms. Some of the wilder, longer varieties arch so high they catch on the lower branches of trees, sending out new branches that reach up farther and farther into the tree. Most often ramblers bloom once in late spring or early summer on year-old canes. Their colors range from pink through red and peach, to yellow and white.

Pillar roses are not as long-stemmed as other roses, but grow more upright with tall, straight, stiffer canes reaching from 5 to 10 feet. They're named pillar roses because they are often planted beside and tied to a formal garden pillar, a lamp post, a support on an arbor, a flagpole, a telephone pole or a fence post. The pillar rose decorates its support, which in turn protects the long canes from wind damage.

'Aloha'
Hybridizer, Date of Introduction: Boerner, 1949
ARS Rating: 7.0
Color: Medium pink
Blooms: 3½ inches, double (55 to 60 petals), R
Fragrance: Strong
Height: 7 to 10 feet
Uses: Pillars, trellis
Characteristics: One of the best climbing hybrid Teas, 'Aloha' is unusual in that there is no true bush form. Dark green, leathery leaves offset abundant rosy pink flowers fully packed with up to 60 petals. Each petal is darker on the outside than inside. 'Aloha' can be prone to mildew.

'America'
Hybridizer, Date of Introduction: Warriner, 1976
ARS Rating: 8.9
Awards: AARS 1976
Color: Orange-pink (coral-salmon)
Blooms: 3½ to 4½ inches, double (40 to 45 petals), R
Fragrance: Strong
Height: 9 to 12 feet
Uses: Trellis, cutting
Characteristics: 'America' is a large-flowered climber and one of only a few climbers to ever receive the AARS award. It has a slight petunia-like fragrance. 'America''s clusters of large, coral-salmon flowers are borne on long stems; it is unusual for a climber to provide excellent cut blooms as 'America' does. It has medium green, semiglossy leaves and is a fair repeat bloomer.

'America' is a climber that is also good as a cut flower.

'American Pillar'

Hybridizer, Date of Introduction: Van Fleet, 1902
ARS Rating:—
Color: Deep pink
Blooms: 2 to 4 inches, single (5 to 7 petals), O
Fragrance: —
Height: 15 to 20 feet
Hips
Disease resistant
Uses: Trellis, gazebo
Characteristics: 'American Pillar' is a rambler with abundant cascades of small, deep pink, single flowers with white eyes that bloom in clusters. It blooms once, late in the rose season, and the flowers are followed by red ornamental hips. The petals, as they brown, cling to the stems like wadded tissue paper, but are easily pulled off to clean the bush. Don't deadhead or you'll lose the hips. 'American Pillar' is very disease resistant because it is a cross between two species, *Rosa wichuraiana* and *R. setigera*.

'Blaze'

Hybridizer, Date of Introduction: Kallay, 1932
ARS Rating: 7.3
Color: Medium red
Blooms: 2½ to 3 inches, semi-double (15 to 20 petals), R
Fragrance: Slight
Height: 8 to 15 feet
Uses: Fences, trellis
Characteristics: 'Blaze' is one of the most popular large-flowered climbers with its long bloom and clusters of bright scarlet, cupped flowers. It is susceptible to black spot and mildew. 'Blaze' can boast the offspring 'Blaze Improved' and 'Blaze

Superior', which may prove to be improved varieties.

'Don Juan'

Hybridizer, Date of Introduction: Maladrone, 1958
ARS Rating: 8.3
Color: Dark red
Blooms: 4½ to 5 inches, double (35 petals), R
Fragrance: Strong
Height: 6 to 10 feet
Disease resistant
Uses: Trellis, pillar
Characteristics: This rose's dark green, leathery and glossy foliage sets off the deep red, velvety flowers. 'Don Juan' is a large-flowered climber. I grow it over a trellis in the herb garden, where it has never been sprayed, even though at summer's end it looks a little ratty. The flowers bloom continuously with wonderful fragrance, and their flavor is so good I candy the petals, shred them on deserts, and boil them for rosewater to flavor custards and other foods. This is a tender climber and not dependably winter-hardy. (Photograph page 80.)

'Eden' ('Pierre de Ronsard'®, 'Eden Rose 88')

Hybridizer, Date of Introduction: Meilland, 1987
ARS Rating:—
Awards: Royal National Rose Society
Color: Pink blend
Blooms: 3 inches, quartered (100+ petals)
Fragrance: Strong
Height: 6 to 8 feet
Uses: Fences, trellis
Characteristics: 'Eden' is a prolific large-flowered climber.

The cup-shaped flowers are packed with more than 115 petals each, pressed flat against each other, almost too numerous to reveal the yellow center. They open with the outer rows of petals a pristine white, in high contrast to the bright, medium pink center, an arresting and unusual combination. As the flower ages, the fragrance lessens, the outer petals relax and the inner petals fade to soft white with a light blush. Each petal has yellow at its base, revealed only if you peek between the petals. The many-petaled flowers hang their heads after a rain but quickly recover when dry. (Photograph page 80.)

'American Pillar' blooms only once, in early summer, but what a spectacular bloom that is.

'Blaze' has clusters of scarlet blooms.

'Don Juan' is a favorite for making rose water and candied rose petals. (See Plant Portrait, page 79.)

'Eden' first opens with a bright, medium pink center that fades to a soft blush. (See Plant Portrait, page 79.)

'New Dawn' has delicate pink flowers.

'Golden Showers' has daffodil yellow flowers.

'Golden Showers'®

Hybridizer, Date of Introduction: Lammerts, 1956
ARS Rating: 7.1
Awards: AARS 1957, Portland gold medal 1957
Color: Medium yellow
Blooms: 3 to 4 inches, double (20 to 35 petals), R
Fragrance: Moderate
Height: 6 to 12 feet
Disease resistant
Uses: Fences, trellis
Characteristics: 'Golden Showers' is a large-flowered climber with daffodil yellow flowers that cover almost thornless canes. It blooms off and on all season in my garden with no special care or feeding.

'Joseph's Coat'®

Hybridizer, Date of Introduction: Armstrong & Swim, 1969
ARS Rating: 7.6
Awards: Bagatelle Gold Metal 1964

'Joseph's Coat' has multicolored blooms.

Color: Red blend
Blooms: 3 to 4 inches, double (24 to 30 petals), R
Fragrance: Slight
Height: 6 to 10 feet
Uses: Landscaping, fences, trellis
Characteristics: As colorful as the name implies, 'Joseph's Coat' is a large-flowered climber that first blooms in midseason, with repeat blooms appearing over the summer. The blossoms open bright yellow flushed with orange and cherry red that gradually darkens to deep red. The clusters of open, cupped blooms are very showy. With pruning, it can be grown as a shrub.

'New Dawn' ('Everblooming Dr. W. Van Fleet', 'The New Dawn')

Hybridizer, Date of Introduction: Dreer, 1930
ARS Rating: 7.1
Color: Light pink
Blooms: 2 to 3½ inches, semi-double (18 to 24 petals), R
Fragrance: Moderate
Height: 12 to 20 feet
Uses: Pillar, trellis, wall
Characteristics: One of the most popular large-flowered climbers, as well as the world's first patented plant, 'New Dawn' is an ever-blooming sport of 'Dr. Van Fleet'. It has heavy bloom in June and can be erratic thereafter, blooming intermittently or not at all in some gardens, all summer long in others. Fall reliably brings a second crop of flowers. This rose is an upright and vigorous large-flowered climber with clusters of cupped, blush pink blooms and showy bright yellow stamens contrasted by dark, glossy green leaves.

PESTS AND DISEASES

NATURE'S WAY

The secret to a healthy garden is in the soil preparation, the regular addition of organic material, the growing of disease-resistant varieties, and keeping a careful watch for pests and disease. Roses in need cry out, and a caring gardener hears. I take healthy gardening farther. I've gone cold turkey on chemical dependence, banning poisons from my garden. Polluting the air and the soil with chemicals and their fumes does not make a healthy garden for my family and friends.

Like thoroughbred horses, many modern roses need pampering and grooming to keep up their performance. They need a gardener's help to prevent infestation and the rapid spread of pests and disease. Is it a compliment to the rose or to the persistence of rosarians that the rose has more pests and diseases given its name? Rose midges, rose scales, rose slugs, rose stem borers, rose galls, rose leaf hoppers, rose mosaic, rose scale and rose weevils are plagues that readily come to mind. The Latin name for black spot is *Diplocarpon rosae*, which includes the scientific name *rosa*. As you can see, there are many pests and diseases that attack roses, and many a rosarian has turned into a near-hypochondriac. Fortunately, not all rose afflictions are prevalent in any area of the country at the same time, and certainly not in the same garden. Besides, many pests and diseases visit for a short while without doing irreversible damage.

Whenever possible, buy disease-resistant varieties of roses. If roses you can't resist are suscepti-ble to diseases, combine them with disease-resistant varieties or perennials, annuals or shrubs to help stop the spread of the problem. There are many things you can do to combat pests and disease without using chemicals, which play dangerous games with your garden's ecosystem. I believe in "tough love," survival of the fittest. Roses that demand too much attention are replaced. This does not mean acting hastily. Many a rose experiences an unhealthy period and then recovers. Weather plays an important part in the health of a rose, and one season is usually too brief a time to adequately judge a rose's success in your garden as many don't look their best until the third year.

Documented evidence on the adverse environmental effects of many toxic products and their long-term health effects on the individuals exposed to them isn't easy to come by. What we do know is that many chemicals are carcinogenic and lethal to both harmful and helpful garden organisms and insects, particularly to the "good" predators such as spider mites, and to fungus. Over time, insects build up immunity to particular chemicals used; outbreaks of mites on roses, for example, can increase noticeably. Chemicals damage rose foliage if misused. An extension agent I know has diagnosed more cases of damage from chemicals than from pests and disease. With chemical use, there is a very fine line between what is helpful and what is harmful.

In our lifetime, we will never know the full effect of chemicals and their repeated use on our

soil, water supply, animals and ourselves. We do know that applications of chemicals, even at low concentrations, pose health problems often. If a chemical is so strong that the manufacturer recommends wearing a protective jumpsuit, goggles, a mask with a filter and rubber gloves when spraying to protect your body, ask yourself if you really want to spray it into the air you breathe, onto the flowers you pick and into your soil. Some rose enthusiasts use chemicals but don't take all the precautions recommended. It is too soon for long-term damage to have been documented, but you shouldn't be among the first cases.

I simply won't risk using chemicals. We drink water from our own well; contaminated water is too big a price to pay for unblemished roses. Weekly sprayings of pesticides and preventive fungicides from spring to fall cause chemical buildup and create an unpleasant odor that masks roses' perfume. If you can smell the pesticide, you're inhaling it into your lungs. Beverly Dobson, one of America's leading rosarians (see page 91) wrote recently, "I have very little black spot or mildew, almost no mildew, in my garden. I can understand the lack of black spot, because I grow mostly old roses and species, but I would think I would have mildew, since so many spots in the lower parts of my garden are boggy and wet most of the year. In the Seventies, when I was exhibiting a lot, I did spray regularly. Since I've stopped, I have less of any diseases or pests. I think this is mainly due to having a mixed garden, that is, mixed plantings, even though roses predominate on all the higher ground."

As I talk to other gardeners, I've seen the mixed garden become a recurrent theme. Planting a large number of roses together is an invitation to a banquet for many pests and creates too happy a breeding ground.

The trend toward using chemicals less is encouraging. Many large public gardens, among them the Brooklyn Botanic Garden and Old Westbury Gardens, use chemicals only occasionally when a problem they can't solve organically arises. This is the stand taken by many extension agencies across the country. Faced with a local anti-pesticide movement, the George E. Owen Municipal Rose Garden in Eugene, Oregon, completely stopped the use of chemical insecticides and fungicides, and in so doing discovered they could still grow beautiful roses. They won the "Outstanding Rose Garden" award from All-American Rose Selections.

PESTICIDES

Pesticides are poisons that destroy and repel pests. They can take many forms: stomach poison, lethal when ingested by the insect; contact poison, which kills on contact with the insect; residual contact poison, which remains toxic to insects, killing them slowly over a period of time; fumigants, which kill when inhaled by insects; systemics, which are absorbed into plants through the leaves or the roots, and travel in its sap, poisoning sucking and chewing insects; and, lastly, repellents that don't kill but are so distasteful insects avoid the area.

Short-term gains in destroying local pests over time become an environmental nightmare as the balance of nature is destroyed. Chemicals build stronger bugs. The bugs that live through an onslaught of chemicals breed increasingly stronger bugs that are even less affected by the chemicals. Rosarians who use chemicals must frequently alternate them to destroy the ever-increasing population of bugs. Systemics don't interfere with the predator balance as much as other chemicals do because they affect only chewing insects. Nevertheless, long-term damage from systemics repeatedly added to the soil is unknown.

Most fungicides are more effective at preventing problems than curing them. They control the growth and propagation of fungi and bacteria on plants. Powdery mildew, rust and black spot are the biggest problems for rose growers. Fungicides can be applied at different times, but are used most commonly as a preventative, sprayed on the plant before any signs of disease appear. Repeated applications, usually weekly, are needed.

Contact fungicides are sprayed when the disease is evident. Any chemical, used repeatedly, will lose its effectiveness. Natural garden fungicides with sulfur as their active ingredient, such as Safers'®, control black spot and powdery mildew without polluting the environment.

DISEASES

The first step toward disease prevention is to understand individual disease cycles, the conditions in which they thrive and the damage they do. Equipped with this knowledge you are more prepared for battle than with all of the chemical warfare available. The organic gardener doesn't have to sit back and accept the fate of the doomed. Still, when disease is prevalent and weather conditions create a perfect breeding ground for disease, it takes more care and closer observation to protect your roses.

Black Spot

IDENTIFICATION: Round black spots, 1/16 inch to 1/2 inch in size, appear. If the infection is mild the spots will remain flecks, causing little damage, but if the disease spreads, the spots will grow together, covering larger areas until the leaf is severely damaged, becomes yellowed on the edges and drops off, defoliating the rosebush by midsummer.

CYCLE: Black spots appear on the leaves three to seven days after the infection takes hold. Spores reproduce every three weeks. The optimum conditions for a black spot infection and plague is rainy, wet weather when the temperature stays between 64° to 75° F. For the disease spores to infect a plant and proliferate, the leaves must be continuously wet for a minimum of seven hours. The rose's food is stored in the leaves and a problem with black spot going into winter can deplete the plant's food supply. It is more of a problem where summers are warm and moist: the Northeast, Southeast and some midwestern states.

PREVENTION: You can't tame the mischief of the rain, but you can control the method of watering. Avoid wetting leaves when watering, or water early in the morning, allowing the leaves time to dry before nightfall. Regularly check young leaves, especially those growing close to the ground, during periods of new growth in spring and fall when temperatures reach the mid 60s and the rainfall and humidity are high. Spores winter over on fallen leaves and in infected canes that have been left in the garden. Rain or sprinklers can splash the spores, spreading disease. Even an unsuspecting gardener can do damage by walking in the garden after heavy rain, inadvertently transporting spores on clothing or tools from one plant to another. Insects and wind carry spores, too. Prune off any damage and dispose of it; don't add it to the compost pile, where the disease can spread.

TREATMENT: Sulfur dust or wettable sulfur in solution used according to the manufacturer's directions is as effective as any chemical fungicide. Don't use sulfur when the temperature is 85° F. or hotter because it may burn the foliage.

Powdery Mildew

IDENTIFICATION: Powdery mildew is rather unsightly, but not a killer. It first makes its presence known in the form of a blister on the top of young leaves. It rarely affects old growth. The blister causes the leaf to curl and exposes the bottom of the leaf to the sun. As the fungus feeds on the plant, it grows into the plant cells just below the epidermis (outer layer). Here it feeds on the sap and kills the cells it invades. It then becomes noticeable as a grayish white, powdery fungus that spots leaves and coats unopened buds. The fungus forms spore sacs as it spreads rapidly. If the infection is severe, the buds never open.

CYCLE: When night temperatures reach 60° F. and the days have overcast skies and temperatures in the 80s, conditions are right for powdery mildew to proliferate. Low light on the leaves when they are coated with a film of water from fog, high humidity or dew promotes the growth of spores, which multiply and produce thousands of new ones every four days. Two days after infection, powdery mildew is visible.

Coastal areas of the country, especially the Pacific Coast, where the temperatures stay moderate and foggy overcast days are common, are where powdery mildew thrives. Minimal rainfall will also increase the problem. Drought-stressed roses are more susceptible. The disease spreads fast.

PREVENTION AND TREATMENT: The spores over winter inside leaf buds and on canes. They can be spread by the wind from plant to plant. During periods of dry weather with temperatures 60° F. and above, check the growing tips, buds and new leaves for signs of powdery mildew. Prune off any infected areas and wash the plants daily with a strong spray of water. At the first sign of infection spray with 3 tablespoons of baking soda per gallon of water, mixed with a spreader-sticker (follow the manufacturer's directions) to help the solution stick to the leaf and not wash off in the rain. (To be efficient, you may add a tablespoon of foliar food to feed the roses.)

RESISTANT ROSES: Wichuraianas, chinas, polyanthas and many red and dark pink roses. Many hybrid Teas are susceptible.

Rust

IDENTIFICATION: Rust is to roses what pimples are to teenagers. Small orange or yellow bumps form on the undersides of leaves, then spread to the top leaves and stems where they become conspicuous. In bad infestations some roses will drop their leaves.

CYCLE: Rainy days with temperatures between 60° and 70° F. are when rust proliferates. The spores reproduce every ten to fourteen days.

PREVENTION: In winter the spores show up as corky, dark blotches on infected canes. Checking the underside of leaves in early spring and pruning any diseased part of the rose helps to prevent the spread of rust. Spores can be spread by wind and water. In areas of the country with hot summers and cold winters nature helps to control rust, but where summers and winters are mild like the Pacific coastal states, rust is a problem.

Canker

IDENTIFICATION: Easy to spot, cankers are enlarged, discolored growths girdling a cane. Many different kinds affect roses, rose canker being the most common. They slow or prevent nutrients and water from passing up and down the cane, and often kill the portion above the center growth.

PREVENTION AND TREATMENT: Poorly drained soil encourages cankers. Check plants when pruning in the spring and cut the diseased area out with sharp pruners sterilized with denatured alcohol.

Fungus-resistant Roses

This list is only a beginning. Check with your local rose society and nurseries. Three classes of roses known for their disease resistance are hybrid musks, hybrid rugosas and shrub roses.

'Ballerina'	'Othello'
'Belinda'	'Pax'
'Belle Story'	'Pretty Jessica'
'Buff Beauty'	'Prosperity'
'Etoile de Hollande'	'Radiance'
'Fimbriata'	Rosa moschata
'F. J. Grootendorst'	Rosa multiflora
'Graham Thomas'	'Therese Bugnet'
'Lady Banks'	'Yellow Lady Banks'
'La Marne'	

INSECTS AND OTHER PESTS

Never spray for pests until you've seen and identified them.

APHIDS: The tender areas below rose buds are favorite meeting places for aphids. As the plant sends sap and nutrients to the developing bud, they feast. These small, pear-shaped, sucking insects, often greenish white, red or black (but sometimes taking on the color of the plant), gather on the most tender plant parts—usually on new growth and the underside of leaves. There they suck plant sap, causing foliage to wither and generally inducing a loss of vigor. They are from barely visible to ¹⁄₁₆ inch long. You will not have trouble seeing them, however, as they enjoy family picnics, attaching to and damaging a plant in groups.

Aphids can carry disease. Worse, they secrete a sweet, sticky substance called "honey dew" that attracts ants and promotes the growth of a fungus known as "black sooty mold." The mold interferes with leaf function, slows photosynthesis, and reduces the plant's vigor.

TREATMENT: Sometimes a fairly strong spray from a hose on the underside of leaves will eliminate these pests. Control with Safer's® Insecticidal Soap made with a natural and biodegradable insecticide formula (available through the Burpee catalogue). Introducing aphids' natural enemies, including ladybugs, lacewings and trichogramma wasps, will relieve the problem.

JAPANESE BEETLES: Japanese beetles are the bane of gardeners east of the Mississippi, and they are spreading west. They'll eat almost anything: leaves, flowers, grass and fruit. Roses are one of their favorite foods and they usually attack the flowers first, leaving good-sized holes. After 30 to 40 days of life, adult beetles lay their eggs in the soil. There the larvae hatch and eat the roots of plants and grass for approximately four months before hibernating for the winter. The next summer they emerge as beetles to continue their attack on plants and fruits.

Beetle traps are available at garden supply stores. These lure beetles with a natural sex attractant, plus a floral scent. The beetles fly into the bag and can't get out. Unfortunately, the traps are so good they attract Japanese beetles from other gardens too, and when I've used them I've invited more problems. A better trap, if you're not squeamish, is a can of water with a thin film of oil or soap suds; flick the slow-moving beetles off the leaves into the jar. They won't be able to fly out.

PREVENTION: You can eliminate the destructive pests while they are living in the lawn or garden, using Safers Grub Killer. This powder contains spores of bacterial *Bacillus popillae* (milky spore disease), toxic only to Japanese beetles and other grubs. It will not harm beneficial insects or pets, and is absolutely safe to handle and easy to use. Best of all, although it takes some time to affect the grub population, it is a long-lasting measure. The spores remain active in the soil for ten years.

LEAFHOPPERS: Wedge-shaped, small and green, gray, or yellow in color, leafhoppers suck juices from the plant and leave it with discolored yellow leaves, stunted growth and buds that do not open. They are also carriers of disease.

PREVENTION AND TREATMENT: Ladybugs, green lacewings and praying mantis love leafhoppers for dinner. Use an

Aphids

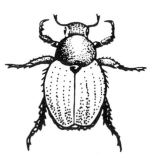

Japanese Beetle

Leafhopper

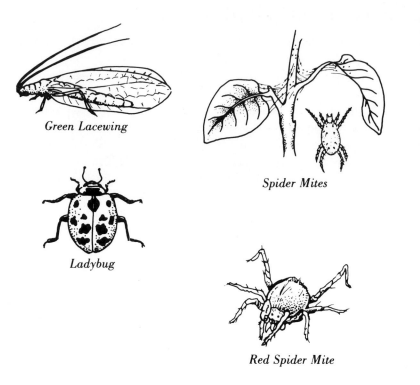

Green Lacewing

Ladybug

Spider Mites

Red Spider Mite

bush in less than 14 days. Warm summer temperatures accelerate their breeding cycle, and they usually do their worst damage before they can be detected.

Chemicals in miticides can do more damage to plants' foliage than mites, because the insects build up resistance over time. A weekly spray of strong water aimed at the underside of leaves, while not 100 percent effective, can reduce a thriving spider mite community and hold off a stampede. A water wand with a "dramm"-type nozzle is specially engineered to combat spider mites.

THRIPS: Thrips are minute (approximately $\frac{1}{20}$ of an inch) winged insects that resemble yellowish brown specks. They hide at the base of rose buds during hot, dry weather. They love the flowers, sucking sap and causing the buds to bend at right angles. They nibble the petal's edges, deforming the flowers and sometimes preventing them from opening. Because thrips do their damage inside the bud, sprays don't easily reach them. It is best to cut off the diseased flower bud when it is first noticed and dispose of it to prevent thrips from multiplying and spreading.

insecticidal soap early in the day when the insects are less active.

PITHBORERS: A number of pests (among them rose stem sawflies, rose stem girdles and carpenter bees) bore into canes, travel down toward the crown (where the stem is grafted onto the roots) and lay their eggs. When the eggs hatch, the larvae eat the pith in the canes, causing damage to the growth between them and the end of the cane. During spring pruning, cut out any infested canes to below the point of infestation, to where the pith is solid white. Seal the fresh cuts with Elmer's glue (see page 35).

SPIDER MITES: Voted "most destructive" of all rose-garden pests by the American Rose Society, spider mites specialize in defoliating a rose-

Pointers for Nonchemical Rose Care

1. *Diet:* A healthy rosebush is best able to ward off pests and disease. A balanced and nutritious diet and two to three inches of water a week are of primary importance (see page 39).

2. *Dormant oil:* Most pests and diseases are not killed by winter weather but wait out the winter in the soil, inside leaf buds and on canes. They are an invisible army, poised and waiting to attack when conditions are right. Spray the entire bush with dormant oil (a nonhazardous, nonpoisonous spray) early in spring before the rose sends out new shoots. Dormant oil is not harmful to the environment. It coats the canes, buds and leaves, suffocating spores of black spot, rust, powdery mildew, and pests such as aphids; unfortunately, it also kills some of the beneficial insects. It will cut down on the need for insecticides during the summer. Prune and discard any diseased area of your rosebush as soon as you notice it.

3. *Pruning:* The most diligent inspectors, like Sherlock Holmes, carry magnifying glasses while regularly inspecting their roses. Prune out all damaged leaves and canes when you see them. Dispose of them where they can't spread disease. Never leave cut stems and leaves lying at the base of the bush or put them in the compost pile. Regularly remove any leaves that wilt or fall from the bush during the growing season. They are probably infected.

4. *Mulch:* Mulching rosebushes in the fall and again in the spring will cover any spores on top of the soil and prevent water from splashing them back onto the rosebush where they can proliferate.

5. *Fertilizing:* Excessive use of chemical fertilizers containing highly soluble nitrogen encourages overproduction of lush, but weak, foliage. Weak new foliage is very susceptible to powdery mildew and, to a lesser degree, rust and black spot.

6. *Watering:* Top-water only when the plant will have time to dry before evening. Both rust and black spot thrive in wet conditions. Powdery mildew, however, can't survive when there is a film of water on the leaves. In the morning, a forceful spray of water directed at both the bottom and the top of the leaves to wash off any mildew spores and aphids during optimum temperatures for powdery mildew production will help control and discourage mildew and aphids without encouraging rust or black spot.

7. *Disease-resistant cultivars:* Plant cultivars that are less susceptible to the diseases and pests common in your area. Contact your local rose society, your local extension office, public garden, or the American Rose Society (see page 91). Gardening friends and neighbors can also recommend their favorite varieties. Some of the most disease-resistant species include *Rosa majalis, R. multiflora, R. rugosa* and *R. wichuraiana.*

6

GARDENERS' MOST-ASKED QUESTIONS

The first Burpee catalog was mailed in 1876, and catalogs have been coming ever since, offering gardeners a wealth of seeds, flowering plants, fruits, shrubs and trees, as well as advice for better gardening. From the earliest years, Burpee has received letters from customers describing their gardens and asking for help with the problems they encounter. Here are the questions more frequently asked of us concerning roses.

PLANTING ROSES

Q. Can roses be moved?
A. Roses can be moved to another spot in the garden, and roses that are not performing well may be dug up and replanted in the same spot with enriched soil and, if necessary, improved drainage. Prune back the top of the rose so the roots have a more manageable job to support the top growth while establishing themselves in their new home. In transplanting, follow the same principles of preparing the soil as for planting a rose (see page 34), watering often for the first few weeks, until the plant puts out new growth. Then you know the roots are established. If you are transplanting in the summer, shade the newly transplanted rose from the bright sun for a few days to prevent dehydration.

Q. When is the best time to move roses?
A. With special care, roses can be moved any time, but the best time to move them is when they are dormant and days and nights are cool. In most areas of the country this is early spring or late fall; in southernmost areas, this is winter. If a rose is moved in midsummer during its growth period, it will be stressed because its roots have been disturbed. In a time of high heat it is difficult for a stressed rose to take up enough water to keep its stems strong. Prune the rose back and remove any flowers before digging it up. Producing blooms takes a great deal of the rose's energy, and it is best to prune the rose back so the bush has less top growth to support while it recovers from its move.

DESIGNING WITH ROSES

Q. Are there any roses that grow in partial shade?
A. It is a mistaken notion that all roses need a full day of sun. While it is true of many modern roses, it is not true of some old-fashioned, species and shrub roses. They can be placed in a partially shady border, grouped along a woodland walk or planted in a woodland clearing where they receive only a half day of sun. For a natural look, group several of the same roses together. They make welcome homes for nesting birds and small animals such as rabbits.

ROSES FOR PARTIAL SHADE
'American Pillar'
Apothecary's Rose
'Ballerina'
'Blanc Double de Coubert'
'Blush Noisette'

Mixing roses with other plants instead of growing them in a bed by themselves will help prevent the spread of disease. Here 'The Fairy' is randomly repeated in a garden of annuals and perennials.

'Complicata'
'Constance Spry'
'Dr. W. Van Fleet'
'Empress Josephine'
'The Fairy'
'F. J. Grootendorst'
'Golden Showers'
'Iceberg'
'Jacques Cartier'
'Max Graf'
'Mme Hardy'
'New Dawn'
'Rosa Mundi'
'Sweet Briar'
'Zéphirine Drouhin'

Q. Which roses are best for the seashore?
A. Roses in the rugosa family adapt readily to seashore and seaside growing (see page 24), and many varieties are available.

Q. What is a landscaping rose?
A. "Landscaping rose" is a new term used by nurserymen to mean a rose that will fit as easily in the landscape as other flowering shrubs. These roses are disease resistant and need no special care.

Q. What is an English rose?
A. This is a name given to a group of roses hybridized by David Austin in England. While not exactly designated as a class—a series would be more accurate—these roses are much talked about. The short time they have been evaluated in this country leads me to be cautious in praise, even though the dozen I have grown for the last few years have not disappointed me. A rose needs to be evaluated over many years and under various climatic conditions.

David Austin of Albrighton, England, has bred for the repeat flowering of disease-resistant shrubs, mixing old shrub roses with modern flowers, many of them clustered flowering varieties such as the floribundas. In many of his creations he has captured old rose fragrance, fully double flowers that repeat bloom, new colors and disease resistance. Many are named after Shakespearean characters and famous English personages.

ENGLISH ROSES POPULAR IN AMERICA

'Abraham Darby'
'Belle Story'
'Constance Spry'
'English Garden'
'Fair Bianca'
'Graham Thomas'
'Heritage'
'Mary Rose'
'Othello'®
'The Reve'®
'Wife of Bath'®

PESTS AND DISEASES

Q. Will the powdery mildew on my lilacs spread to my roses?
A. No; the disease is host-specific, which means the mildew that affects the lilac is different than the mildew that affects roses.

Q. Why is powdery mildew so much more damaging to my roses than to lilacs?
A. On lilacs powdery mildew generally shows up after the lilacs have bloomed. On roses, powdery mildew attacks the flower buds before they open and hurts the bloom.

Q. Are there hybrid Tea roses resistant to powdery mildew?
A. Resistant hybrid Tea varieties include: 'Aztec', 'Duet', 'Fragrant Cloud', 'Olympiad', 'Queen Charlotte', 'Santa Fe', 'Smooth Lady', Floribundas, 'Acapulco', 'Fire King', 'Impatient', 'Spartan' and 'Sunsprite'. Grandifloras resistant to powdery mildew are: 'Camelot', 'Montezuma', 'Mount Shasta', 'Pink Parfait' and 'Queen Elizabeth'.

Check your Burpee catalog for Safer's and Ringer's products to keep your garden healthy.

CUTTING ROSES

Q. Why can't I grow long-stemmed roses like the ones I buy from the florist?
A. Florist roses are hybrid Tea roses, grown in greenhouses and pruned and groomed specifically for their long stems. Most florist roses would not make good garden plants. Rosarians growing roses for exhibiting at rose shows around the country are growing roses for the same characteristics as the florist roses. You could try a few of their tricks. A horizontal cane will send up tall straight stems at each leaf node. To produce a long stem on a rose

that doesn't produce long stems naturally, peg down a cane by gently forcing it into as horizontal a position as possible and, if it is close to the ground, use horseshoe-shaped pegs or wire to hold it down. If the cane is near a fence, it could be tied to the fence to hold its horizontal position, or poles could be placed in a line and the cane tied from one to another. Disbudding (removing all side buds and side shoots on a cane to allow the main, top bud to develop) will produce one large flower. Without disbudding, more flowers develop on each stem, but often of a smaller size and inferior quality.

Q. At what stage should I cut roses for them to last the longest?
A. Generally, cutting roses in the bud stage will give you longer life, but this varies with the rose. Roses with single flowers can be cut in a "tight" bud covered with green sepals, and they will open when placed in water. The semidouble and double flowers should be cut when the bud has started to unfold its flower, or the bud might not open in water. However, buds can be enjoyed in water for several weeks and then air dried to be used in winter arrangements.

Q. Can I grow roses from seed?
A. It depends on the rose. Species roses can be grown from seed and will come true to their family, but not necessarily the same as their parent.

Q. Where can I find rare and old-fashioned roses?
A. In *The Combined Rose List.* This booklet, published yearly, is a source list of all commercially available roses including rare and unusual varieties, and it lists rose organizations too. It is compiled by Peter Schneider and Beverly Dobson. To order one, write to Peter Schneider P.O. Box 16035, Rocky River, OH 44116;
or call Beverly Dobson at (914) 591-6736.

Q. How can I keep up-to-date on the latest introductions and methods of growing good roses?
A. There are many rose organizations that publish newsletters and magazines to help keep readers current. For information about them, consult your local rose society or write to:

The American Rose Society
P.O. Box 30,000
Shreveport, LA 71130
Dues: $32.00
Publishes a soft-bound annual and a monthly magazine

Heritage Rose Foundation
Charles A. Walker Jr.
1512 Gormon Street
Raleigh, NC 27606
(919) 834-2591
Dues: $10
Publishes a quarterly newsletter

Texas Rose Rustlers
9426 Kerrwood
Houston, TX 77080
(713) 464-8607
Dues: $7
Publishes a quarterly newsletter

Write or call for a free Burpee catalog:
W. Atlee Burpee & Company
300 Park Avenue
Warminster, PA 18974
(215) 674-9612

"Rose Rustlers"

Many old varieties that have fallen from commerce have been rediscovered growing in graveyards, near abandoned houses and along roadsides where they have lived for years on their own, without any special tending. Groups of "rose rustlers," as they call themselves, scour roadsides, vacant lots and old cemeteries looking for old bushes from which they gather cuttings to propagate the roses. In doing so, they promote more vigorous roses.
Tom Christopher is a wonderful rosarian storyteller, and his book, In Search of Lost Roses, *tells many a tale of the rediscovery of glorious old roses.*

THE USDA
PLANT
HARDINESS
MAP
OF THE
UNITED
STATES

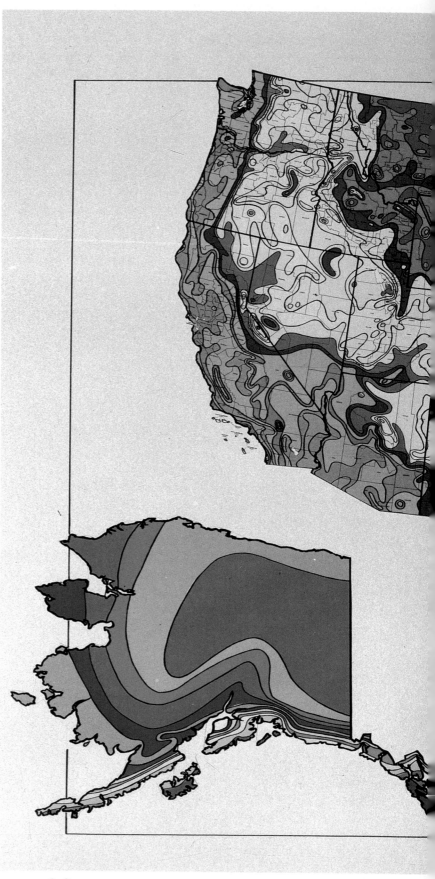

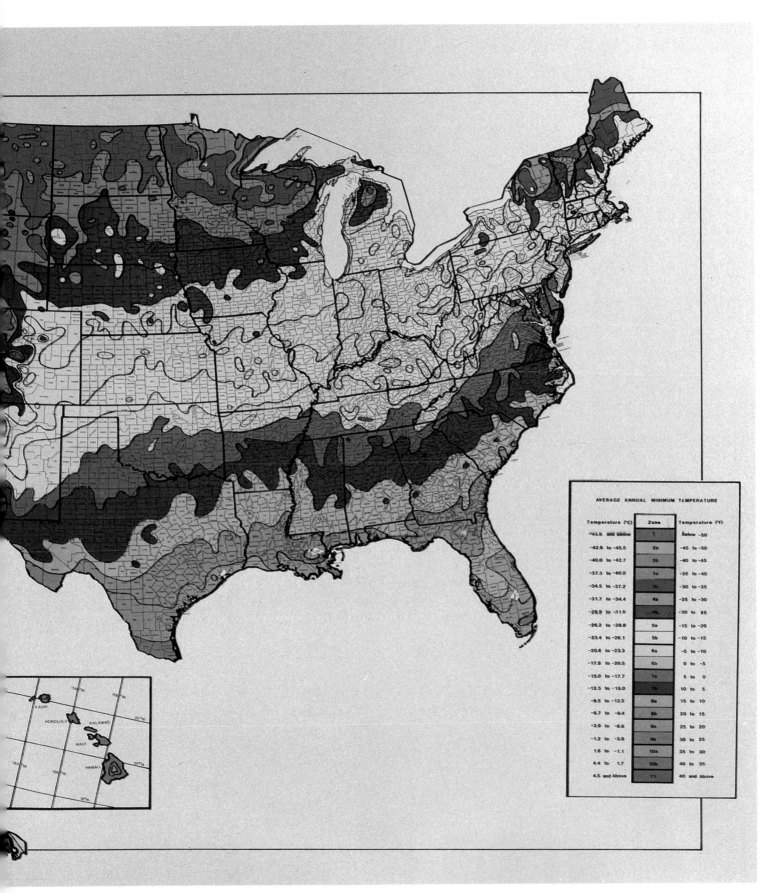

AVERAGE ANNUAL MINIMUM TEMPERATURE

Temperature (°C)	Zone	Temperature (°F)
-45.6 and below	1	Below -50
-42.8 to -45.5	2a	-45 to -50
-40.0 to -42.7	2b	-40 to -45
-37.3 to -40.0	3a	-35 to -40
-34.5 to -37.2	3b	-30 to -35
-31.7 to -34.4	4a	-25 to -30
-28.9 to -31.6	4b	-20 to -25
-26.2 to -28.8	5a	-15 to -20
-23.4 to -26.1	5b	-10 to -15
-20.6 to -23.3	6a	-5 to -10
-17.8 to -20.5	6b	0 to -5
-15.0 to -17.7	7a	5 to 0
-12.3 to -15.0	7b	10 to 5
-9.5 to -12.2	8a	15 to 10
-6.7 to -9.4	8b	20 to 15
-3.9 to -6.6	9a	25 to 20
-1.2 to -3.8	9b	30 to 25
1.6 to -1.1	10a	35 to 30
4.4 to 1.7	10b	40 to 35
4.5 and Above	11	40 and Above

INDEX

(Note: Italized page numbers refer to captions)

Cut along dotted line.

Cut along dotted line.

000646